BLACK FAMILY ENTERPRISE AND COMMUNITY IN SEGREGATED NORTH OMAHA

Dr. Valandra

BLACK FAMILY ENTERPRISE AND COMMUNITY IN SEGREGATED NORTH OMAHA

The Pratt Street House

The Black Studies Collection

Collection Editor
Dr Christopher McAuley

LPp

For my ancestors

Great-great-great-grandparents Lizzy Spotsell Johnson and
Jim Singleton

Great-great maternal grandparents Willie Ann Rogers and
Jim Henderson

Great-great paternal grandparents Monroe Hall and
Anna Sayers Hall

Great-grandparents Ida Henderson Hall and Dennis Hall

Grandparents Berdine Hall Williams and Bobby Williams

First published in 2024 by Lived Places Publishing

The authors and editors have made every effort to ensure the accuracy of information contained in this publication, but assume no responsibility for any errors, inaccuracies, inconsistencies or omissions. Likewise, every effort has been made to contact copyright holders. If any copyright material has been reproduced unwittingly and without permission the Publisher will gladly receive information enabling them to rectify any error or omission in subsequent editions.

Copyright © 2024 Lived Places Publishing

British Library Cataloguing in Publication Data
A CIP record for this book is available from the British Library

ISBN: 9781915734624 (pbk)
ISBN: 9781915734648 (ePDF)
ISBN: 9781915734631 (ePUB)

The right of Valandra to be identified as the Authors of this work has been asserted by them in accordance with the Copyright, Design and Patents Act 1988.

Cover design by Fiachra McCarthy
Book design by Rachel Trolove of Twin Trail Design
Typeset by Newgen Publishing UK

Lived Places Publishing
Long Island
New York 11789

www.livedplacespublishing.com

Abstract

This interpretative account of a working-class Black community in North Omaha illustrates the common and unique ways residents claim space and place in defining their lives and community and sustaining their histories, culture, and traditions. These stories of Black urban placemaking address themes of mutual aid, safety, religion, activism, caregiving, structural inequality, and injustice. Black family enterprise and industry are explored through the lived experiences of the author's grandparents and interviews with former and current residents of North Omaha. These intergenerational stories of individual, family, and community resilience and determination demonstrate how ideological, historical, economic, and sociopolitical forces converge to create barriers and opportunities that influence living in a segregated urban community.

Key words

Black family enterprise; segregation; housing; religion; residential caregiving; community; highway construction; gentrification; urban planning; development and disinvestment.

Acknowledgments

Bobby and Berdine Williams

This book reflects a collective effort on the part of family and friends who supported, encouraged, and inspired me generously in ways for which I am forever grateful and appreciative. First and foremost, I honor my ancestors for their steadfastness in weathering unfathomable conditions for generations that

I might walk less burdened in this world. Thank you. I am equally grateful for the sustained support and guidance of my mother, Ida Frazer; sisters, Jendayi Frazer and Ramona Durham; companion, RoAnne Elliott; and Aunt Doris M. Williams. Your unwavering love, support, and insights lighted my way through this journey, providing the fuel to see it through.

Several friends rooted for me, offering encouraging words of support, and visited with Grandma. Thank you, Sandra S.Alcaparras, Angela Yeong, Anne McInerny, Robbin Frazier, Nancy Lee, Sara Summers, Anne Shelley and Bridget Gibson, Kameri Christy, Ananda Rosa, LaShawnda Fields, Romona West, Priscilla Gibson, Pattie Williams, and Katherine Brill. This book began to take shape in my writing group, and I thank RoAnne, Dorothy Dodson Marcy, Rashauna "Coco" Hintz, and Marteka Landrum for patiently listening and providing me with critical feedback.

Thank you to all of Grandma's grand- and great-grandchildren, Jeanelle, Shinaye, "Berdie," Michael, Mimi, nieces and nephews in Omaha, her niece Ms. Evalina Williams and grandniece Rosiland Leon in Brinkley, for helping with Grandma's care and staying in touch with her regularly. I want to also thank Richard Partee, our family friend, for honoring Grandpa's wish to help Grandma in Omaha and for all of the trips you made to visit her in Arkansas. Thank you to the certified nursing aids, Javon, Mylina, and Kassie, for your patience and assistance caring for Grandma.

The rich, nuanced stories of Black life presented here would not have been possible without the willingness of long-term residents of North Omaha to share their lives graciously. It was a tremendous joy to reconnect with my childhood friends Suzanne

"Susie" Tarver, Barbara, and Milton Tarver after 40 years and to make a new friend, Linda Hill. Mount Moriah Baptist Church has held a special spiritual place in my family for generations. I am grateful for the time spent with pastor Reverend T. Michael Williams, learning about his ministry and activist work in Omaha. I also want to acknowledge my cousin Tracy and her parents, Mrs. Ruby and Mr. Sidney Smith. Growing up in the 28th and Pratt Street neighborhood, they played a significant role in my life. Finally, I want to thank Lynette D'Amico for her wisdom and guidance in getting the ball rolling and the editorial team at Lived Places Publishing for a supportive editorial process.

Notes on language

1. I use the terms Black and African American interchangeably.

2. I capitalize both Black and White as racial designations except when quoting previously published scholarship. The capitalization of Black and White people acknowledges that both groups are racialized through the processes of white domination. It also disrupts the depiction of whiteness as normative, making it more visible as a significant factor in the historical and contemporary experiences of people based on their racialization as Black or White.

3. I use the term enslaved instead of slave, except in quoting previously published scholarship, to recognize Black people's humanity and acknowledge the racial oppression used by the white power structure in the United States to deny Black people their freedom by placing them in bondage to exploit their labor and suppress their lives.

4. I use the term white power structure to represent laws, policies, and customs created and enacted by a majority White public to systemically disenfranchise Black voters, curtail Black freedom, and otherwise restrict Black economic, political, and social progress. Regardless of race, people in positions of power can enact these policies.

5. I use quotes from my great-great-grandmother, Willie Ann Roger's Federal Writers' Project (FWP) Slave Narrative interview with Irene Robertson, a White woman who prepared 97 per cent (290/300) of the narratives from the Arkansas

FWP interviews in the counties of Crittenden, Philips, Monroe, Lee, Moro, St. Francis, and Prairie. Historians have criticized the FWP interviews for many reasons, including how White interviewers construct "Black speech" using degrading, patronizing minstrel depictions and spellings that make Black people sound ignorant, backward, and living in calm contentment. To counter these negative depictions, I followed the lead of historian Emberton (2022) and standardized the written dialect and spelling of the quotes to minimize distractions and maximize meaning. However, growing up in a family with Southern roots, there are certain words, phrases, and expressions that I have come to associate with the South, but not exclusively with Black people in the South, and in these instances, I did not change the speech or phrasing of the quotes. For example, phrases like "I reckon."

Contents

Learning objectives   xiii

Introduction   1

  Motivation   4

  Methodology   7

Part I: History   11

Chapter 1 Southern roots and migration North   13

Chapter 2 History of North Omaha   33

Part II: Community pillars   55

Chapter 3 The Williams Residential Care Home   57

Chapter 4 The Tarver family   79

Chapter 5 Reverend T. Michael Williams   97

Chapter 6 Linda Hill   117

Part III: Neighborhood, inheritance, and legacy   129

Chapter 7 History of the North Freeway
and city planning   131

Chapter 8 Berdine Hall Williams   141

Conclusion   177

Suggested discussion topics   186

References   187

Further reading   192

Index   193

Learning objectives

- What are the diverse ways a community is self-defined and enacted?
- What acts of community, enterprise, resilience, resistance, and refusal are represented?
- What are the intergenerational impacts of housing history and urban development policies and practices?
- In what ways can practitioners collaborate with communities for equity?
- How do Northern segregated communities reflect Southern Jim Crow policies and practices?
- How do interpersonal experiences shape your understanding of and construction of what constitutes home, community, neighborhood, and city beyond geographical boundaries?
- How do the intersections of race, class, and culture shape community cohesiveness?
- In what ways can neighborhood integration be beneficial or harmful?

Introduction

It was the day after Christmas in 1980, almost 30 years after my grandparents, Bobby and Berdine Hall Williams, bought the Pratt Street house, when we were sitting around the festively laid table after dinner, and my then 60-year-old grandmother said,

> I'm not saying it because I was born and raised there, but if I could have lived there, I would have never left Arkansas. I'd stayed there and built in my own birth-place, had my name printed up on the building—"Built by Bobby and Berdine Williams," you know what I mean, instead of here in Omaha.

As if responding to an unspoken question of why Arkansas, she explained further, "Because, honey, that was where I was born and raised, and I never will say I was born anywhere else because I'm not gonna tell a lie. I love my birthplace, but my health caused me to leave that place."

The staunch pride in her voice startled me. Unlike Grandpa, who was also born in Arkansas and talked about his life there read-ily and, seemingly, with greater ease, Grandma rarely did. "You know," she continued,

> After I came here, I got better, but I couldn't cope with this prejudice when I came to Omaha. I kept my Bible

with me night and day, and I still do. If I don't read my Bible every night, I have to read my Bible every morning. Every morning before leaving for work, I get on my knees and pray. Ask the Lord to bless all races, all creeds, and all colors because you know we can't get to heaven having hatred in our hearts.

I listened attentively. Feelings of pride and sadness bubbled up in me. I felt pride in hearing the determination in my grandmother's voice and sadness at the prejudice she and my grandpa had endured.

As we helped Grandma clear the dishes and remaining food from the table, I wondered what fueled her steadfast determination, faith, and vision. I wondered whether her health was the only reason she left Arkansas and if there were other reasons she did not want to share at that moment. Faith and prayer sustained my grandparents in their efforts to build a better life for themselves and their family while weathering the ongoing storms of racial prejudice and discrimination. Nevertheless, I was curious about what else helped them thrive in the face of racism and housing discrimination when they arrived in Omaha in 1944.

I wondered how they overcame the prejudices Grandma had not explicitly named to buy and later convert their Pratt Street house into a licensed residential care home for their community in 1954 and purchased two residential homes in 1972 to provide semi-independent living for adults. In 1977, they built a $600,000, single-level, 60-bed nursing home, the Williams Care Manor, at 3525 Evans Street in North Omaha, a family enterprise that employed and served people of all races, creeds, and colors, as

Grandma said. I learned the answers to some of these questions and much more throughout my life. Their diligence and persistence were evident in all they accomplished. The Williams Care Manor was sold in 1992 after serving the North Omaha community for 38 years. Grandma, however, continued her dream of providing health care to adults, working into her late 90s with her youngest daughter Doris Williams.

Grandma's work ethic and motto were, "I will retire when God retires me." She closed her eyes for the last time in November 2020, dying peacefully in her sleep at my home in Arkansas, her birthplace, when she was 101 years old. I was her legal guardian. Sixty years earlier, in November 1960, when I opened my eyes for the first time in Omaha, NE, my birthplace, she became my guardian angel, teaching me the meaning of home and community in words and deeds.

This interpretive account of a working-class Black community in segregated North Omaha explores my grandparents' life after they migrated from rural Arkansas to Nebraska in 1944. By 1952, they bought a two-story, five-bedroom white house on the corner of Pratt and 28th Street in North Omaha and, two years later, converted it into a residential care home where they lived with their five children, and cared for five adult women. The Pratt Street house is one story of a Black family and community and their relationship to home. The neighborhood residents' everyday experiences of the 28th Street block between Pratt and Pinkney Streets illustrate African American traditions of intergenerational business enterprise, resistance, resilience, and determination. Through first-person interviews with former and current North Omaha residents and personal reflections from my own life, this story illuminates how homeownership, entrepreneurship, mutual aid, and faith created a beacon of light and a sanctuary of safety and security in an urban segregated setting.

These narratives of Black urban place-making emphasize migration patterns, geography, and relatedness through culture, leisure, work, life, and living defined by the residents. They disrupt commonly held assumptions that Black urban spaces lack community stewardship and heritage preservation. They disrupt the constructions of Black people in urban spaces as dangerous, criminals, and unwelcoming. In summary, I illustrate the common and unique ways Black residents in the 28th Street neighborhood and the Near North Side of Omaha claim space and place in defining their lives and community and sustaining their traditions. Finally, I demonstrate how racism, housing segregation, and city disinvestment affected individual and community life and aspirations and explore what helped residents live with and resist racial and economic injustice.

Motivation

Deficit-based framing of Black urban life

In the early days of my teaching career, I cringed at the inaccurate, oversimplified, and offensive representations of black life I regularly observed in textbooks intended to "help" prepare students for human service practice with Black families. These representations constructed Black family and community life as deficient, deviant, problematic, and dysfunctional. Case study narratives habitually depicted many unfavorable characteristics and landscapes framed as endemic to Black family values, traditions, and geography. Negative statistics overpowered descriptions of families' experiences living in urban, low-income, and economically mixed neighborhoods, even in textbooks that purported to use a strength-based, culturally sensitive approach.

Frustrated and disappointed, I attempted to console myself with thoughts like, "I'm thankful that I grew up in a Black neighborhood and know better than that." It was not enough to say this to myself, however. I needed to change the script for the larger audience of students I was responsible for teaching. Enveloped by Eurocentrically-driven academic and professional practice settings necessitated an ongoing critical consciousness, commitment, and diligence of effort to counter the Black pathology gushing through the pages of texts. I wanted to see the Black working-class values, cultural assets, and heritage that I grew up with reflected in those textbooks' stories of Black life. Representation matters. I wanted the multi-generational family practices and traditions that nurtured me to loom as prominent on the page as the blemishes and challenges shaping and reflecting the human experience.

As an interdisciplinary scholar of Black studies and social work, I spent a tremendous amount of time during my teaching career urgently seeking resources that, at a minimum, offered students a more complex and nuanced depiction of Black urban landscapes and working-class communities with limited success. These efforts profoundly shape the foundation of my research practice and scholarship today. Equally, I am guided by my embodied experiences and memories of living in North Omaha for roughly 20 years and visiting my grandparents there for almost 40 years as an adult.

I spent the first five years of my life and subsequent summers with my grandparents at the 2801 Pratt Street house. After high school, I returned to Omaha as a 17-year-old. I lived with them at North 39th Street while attending college and graduate school in business administration at the University of Nebraska-Omaha. I lived in the area off 50th and Ames in North Omaha for another ten years until 1988, after graduating with a master's in business administration. Since then, I have returned to North Omaha to visit my grandparents for holidays, birthdays, and other special events or occasions. I lived roughly 20 years in North Omaha and still consider the area home. I was baptized as a child and attended Mount Moriah Baptist Church, the same church my grandparents were members of for 75 years.

Like many other families living on the 28th Street block between Pratt and Pickney Streets, my grandparents were hardworking, religious, value-driven folk who migrated from the rural South. Their grandparents lived through the aftermath of the Civil War and the legacy of racial violence through Reconstruction. They had first-hand experience living in the racially repressive Jim Crow South. They brought many of their traditions, memories, and stories to the racially segregated urban centers of the North. Through listening and observations, I learned as they transmitted their values, beliefs, spirituality, and approach to living to me and subsequent generations through oral traditions, instructions, and deeds. Many of their neighbors had also traveled similar roads North for different reasons and some of the same. However, their everyday experiences and stories of settlement into urban Black life in the North were missing from the dominant, often distorted discourses of Black life and urban geographies found in textbooks.

Black families are the heart of the Black community in North Omaha. How families and friends looked out for one another, supported each other financially, spiritually, and emotionally, and held each other accountable created an enclave of community resistance and security most of the time. Many families worked outside of the racially segregated community but also cultivated, out of necessity and interest, entrepreneurial enterprises within the Black community that sustained us all and provided direction, hope, and inspired confidence in living in a white-dominated world. Some problems also challenged community cohesiveness. However, as a child of a military family that relocated frequently, spending my summers in Omaha with my grandparents was a source of stability that grounded me and sustained me throughout my life. In this work, I share the stories of some Black families and institutions that cultivated life in Omaha on the Near North Side.

Methodology

I use a combination of autoethnographic, oral history interviews, and archival research methods to illustrate the rich and complex lives of the families living in the Pratt Street house neighborhood and North Omaha. Autoethnography is a qualitative method of research that combines the study of one's own life experiences and the study of the cultural practices and customs of others, typically conducted through interviews and observations and self-reflection or reflexive analysis (Valandra, 2012; Winkler, 2018). I also rely on the work of scholars Saidiya Hartman and Toni Morrison to help me deal with the gaps in the recorded historical records of my ancestors' lives. Hartman uses a method she refers to as "critical fabulation" (Hartman, 2008, p. 11), which combines historical and fictional accounts to re-imagine narratives of the agency of Black women without ignoring their subjugation when there are gaps in the written records. Toni Morrison used a method she described as "literary archeology" (Morrison, 2008, p. 71) to access the interior life of enslaved people. She noted that as a Black writer and woman writing about a time when her ancestors lived, she could embrace autobiographical strategies and reconstruct the world that the gaps implied.

My great-great-grandmother Willie Ann Rogers' industry and service to her community in Arkansas was known to my family early in my life because my grandmother Berdine often talked about how she would travel with her grandmother, Willie Ann, to help deliver babies and attend to sick people in her rural community in Wheatley and Brinkley, Arkansas. Those experiences inspired my grandmother to want to become a doctor. This oral autobiographical knowledge provided context for me as I interpreted the Federal Writers' Project (FWP) transcript of an interview with Willie Ann when she was 70 (Robertson and Rogers, 1938).

Dialogue from interviews I held with former and current residents of North Omaha and those who live on the 28th Street block between Pratt and Pinkney Streets is also used to tell the family stories in this book. The voices of neighborhood residents amplify family intimacies, intricate relational neighborhood interactions, and minute details of daily urban living, offering a fuller, more diverse, and contextually layered picture beyond my summer childhood memories and the time I lived in North Omaha as an adult. Hundreds of hours of tape-recorded and videotaped interviews with my grandparents, especially my grandmother, throughout their adult lives and recorded interviews with relatives, especially my mother Ida and Aunt Doris, and those who knew my grandparents also shape the dialogue presented in this book. I also analyzed family photos, newspaper articles, public records, and other secondary sources to provide historical context and illustrate community life germinating over four decades. Historical documents—census records, land deeds, marriage licenses, birth and death certificates—including a transcript of an interview with my great-great-grandmother Willie Ann Rogers by the Works Progress Administration's (WPA) FWP Slave Narratives help tell this story. The names in this book include the actual names of the people described, and some fictionalized names are used to maintain anonymity when necessary.

PART I
History

Chapter 1
Southern roots and migration North

Writing about the places that raised us, award-winning author Kephart (2021, p. 1) proposed that "We have been shaped by the houses and the land of our past. We remember, through them, what we have gained and what we have lost, what we were offered and what we were denied, what we have decided about transience, permanence, and most things in between." Like generations of Black Americans, my life and that of my ancestors are shaped, in part, by our collective resistance to institutions of enslavement and ongoing oppression and our unwavering insistence on demanding our rights to live as full citizens in the United States.

My great-great-great-grandmother Lizzie Spotsell Johnson's long walk from enslavement in Richmond, Virginia, to relative freedom in Friars Point, Mississippi, in 1861 exemplifies our persistence and determination. Lizzie is part of what Emberton (2022 p. xix) calls the "charter generation of freedom"—people with direct experiences of enslavement and emancipation and its prolonged aftermath. Based on family records and the FWP interview of Willie Ann, it is estimated that Lizzie was born in 1834, sold away from her family at about 14 years old, and lived 27 years of her life enslaved in Richmond, Virginia until she escaped in around 1861 when Union soldiers entered Richmond at the dawning of the Civil War.

In the African American oral tradition, Lizzie shared parts of her life history with her daughter, Willie Ann. At 70 years old, Willie Ann narrated it to Irene Robertson when Irene showed up in the rural farm community of Monroe County, two miles east of Brinkley, Arkansas, in 1938. The transcript of Willie Ann's interview with Robertson tells a complex story of intergenerational faith, courage, and determination in surviving what Emberton (2022) described as several different Souths—the enslavement South, the wartime South, the Reconstruction South, and the Jim Crow South.

It is an intergenerational family story of a collective life history that spans roughly 186 years (1834–2020) and challenges prevailing narratives of whiteness as innocent, superior, objective, and benign. Over time, these mythical narratives have been framed as historical facts and used to maintain, camouflage, and perpetuate racist ideologies and a racial caste system firmly anchored in America's political, economic, and sociocultural landscapes. The intergenerational story of my ancestors' lives offers me a window into my identity and life in proximity to Black human geographies in the South and the North and overarching structures of power, privilege, and oppression.

The enslaved South

Willie Ann was born three years after the end of the Civil War in 1868. When Robertson knocked on her door in 1938, 70 years later, Willie Ann explained the situation surrounding her birth record as her mother Lizzie had related it to her:

> I was born three years after the surrender. I was born in Friars Point, Mississippi. The reason I don't know the exact date when I was born, my ma put it down in the Bible, and the house burned up, and everything in it burned to ashes. She found someone who could write nice to write all the names and ages for her.

Willie Ann would remain in Friars Point with her family until 1880, when they moved to Helena, Arkansas, where my great-grandmother Ida Hall Henderson was born. Willie Ann did not share much about her life as a child in Mississippi except to say that she had four or five sisters who all died and that her mother married in Mississippi as a relatively free woman after literally walking away from enslavement in Richmond, Virginia, described as one of the largest and most profitable slave-trading centers near the central commercial district of Wall Street in the antebellum South outside of New Orleans between 1800 and 1860 (Trammell, 2012).

It is virtually impossible to know how old Willie Ann was when Lizzie decided to share her life story with her daughter or why. However, Willie Ann did remember it and conveyed it to Robertson like this:

> When Ma was a young woman, she said they put her on a block and sold her. They auctioned her off in Richmond, Virginia. When they sold her, her mother fainted or dropped dead; she never knew which. She wanted to see her mother lying over there on the ground, and the

man who bought her wouldn't let her. He just took her on. Drove her off like cattle. The man that bought her was Ephram Hester. That is the last she ever knew of any of her folks.

In *The Weeping Time: Memory and the Largest Slave Auction in American History*, historian Bailey asserts that enslaved people experienced the auction block as the end of life as they knew it. It represented "a kind of death since separation from loved ones was most often permanent" (2017, p. 29).

What might have been Lizzie's intentions in sharing her specific experience with her daughter? What did this mother want to convey and pass on to her daughter? Mothers exercise some autonomy and agency in deciding when and what they will and will not share with their offspring. They can be motivated by many things, including transmitting family traditions or teaching valuable lessons. Mothers sometimes share stories about their life experiences to protect and shield their children and keep them out of harm's way when possible. Storytelling about one's life can also be a mother's way of expressing or demonstrating love when little else can be shown or tangibly given. When Lizzie's bond with her mother was severed, what could Lizzie hold on to, *re*-member—put back together, that she might share with her children in a context when her autonomy and agency were severely limited and subjugated?

After Union soldiers entered Richmond, Virginia, at the onset of the Civil War in 1861, Lizzie left the land of her enslaver, chasing after her son Mose Kent, the only child she was known to have while enslaved. Perhaps compelled by the threat of separation from another loved one or the painful memory of what her mother could not do for her when she was put up for auction, Lizzie did not hesitate to drop whatever she was doing or stop to gather any belongings she might have managed to acquire; she followed Mose with only the clothes on her back and the memories of her kin that she held onto like treasures for the next generation to inherit.

Willie Ann told the FWP interviewer,

> When it was time for freedom, a whole army of Yankees came by and saw Mose working. They told him that if he goes with them, they will give him a spotted horse and a pair of red boots. He crawled up on the horse and was gone. Lizzie started right after them, following him day and night. She nearly starved, just begged along the road all she could. I heard her say how fast she had to walk to keep on their trail and how many nights. She said some nights when they camped, she would beg around and try to fill up. But she couldn't get to Mose without them seeing her. When they got to Friars Point, she went and got him. They just laughed and never gave him anything.

Conventional narratives about Union soldiers often depict them as sympathetic to the plight of Black people and opposed to slavery. However, Lizzie's experience with them would suggest otherwise. In her research on White women as enslavers in the American South, historian Jones-Rogers (2019) recognized that throughout the war, many northern soldiers treated African Americans, free and enslaved, with contempt and held denigrating beliefs about them like their southern counterparts.

In addition, she noted, "Union soldiers and officers stole from enslaved people, raped and brutalized them, sold them and pocketed the profits, and kept enslaved people for themselves" (p. 153). Historian Feimster (2005) explained that public acts that demonstrated power over Black people, including the public rape of Black women, were used by some Union soldiers to remind enslavers of their dwindling authority, mark Southern defeat, and symbolize Union victory. Union troops used Friars Point, a port town on the Mississippi River, as a headquarters and rendezvous point for its transport ships. Hence, Lizzie and her family likely continued to encounter them. While occupying the town, Union troops burned portions of it, possibly including the house Willie Ann mentioned in explaining the loss of her birth records to Robertson.

Once in Friars Point, Willie Ann shared that "Lizzie married at Friars Point. She had just one boy, and I had four or five sisters. They are all dead except me and Mose. He thinks he is about 90 years old. He came here [Brinkley] to see me last year. He sure is feeble." It is unclear how long after Lizzie and Mose arrived in Mississippi that Lizzie lived as a relatively free woman after the wartime South, with a husband of her choosing and a little more autonomy over her own body in deciding when she would bear children. Still, Lizzie's husband, Jim Singleton, Willie Ann's father, likely found work wherever he could, like many recently emancipated men. Lizzie probably continued to do domestic work, perhaps like the work she did while enslaved. Willie Ann recalled, "When Ephram Hester bought [her mother], they taught her to work about the house. She cooked and swept and knocked flies and tended to the children. She stayed with them a pretty long time until she ran off and went to Friars Point." The roughly 20-year age difference between Mose and Willie Ann suggests that Lizzie was enslaved for about 27 years.

It appears they lived in Mississippi for at least 12 to 14 years based on what Willie Ann shared about her birth in 1868 and the time of her daughter's birth, my great-grandmother Ida, in 1880, 12 years later, in Helena, Arkansas. Based on the entries in our family Bible, Willie Ann had two more children: a daughter named Lizzie Henderson but called L.C., who died in 1920, and a son, Sherman Henderson, who died in 1964, possibly named after Union General William T. Sherman.

The reconstruction South

The period of Reconstruction (1865–1877) has been described as a "time of bewildering contradictions" (Emberton, 2022, p. 51), offering great promise for fundamental political, economic, and social reforms in the lives of formerly enslaved Black people (Barnes, 2004; Gordon, 1993). Simultaneously, thousands of Black women, men, and children were placed at significant risk for racial and political violence by "countless white people [who] participated in attacking and killing Black people to defend white supremacy" (Equal Justice Initiative, 2020, p. 28). For example, an attack occurred in 1875 in Friars Point when Lizzie and her family lived there. To regain political power over Black Republicans and suppress the Black vote, former Confederate Brigadier General James Alcorn led a posse of armed White men to attack and kill Black people (Rable, 2007).

Meanwhile, the Arkansas Delta was gaining a reputation as "the promised land" (Gordon, 1993, p. 98) after the Civil War and the beginning of Reconstruction. This perception was fueled, in part, by the state's history and geography. As a border state on the outer edge of the slave South, many Blacks perceived Arkansas as a place of economic and political opportunity (Gordon, 1993). Additionally, labor agents employed by White Delta planters enticed Black people to move to Arkansas, promising them more fertile soil and wages 33–50 per cent higher than in states like Tennessee, South Carolina, and Georgia (Matkin-Rawn, 2013). Furthermore, the enslavement of Black people in Arkansas was primarily concentrated in the Delta region; by 1860, 61 per cent of the enslaved population lived there. Thus, Blacks exercised significant political power in the Delta region during Reconstruction, attracting a large Black migration from southeastern states into Arkansas in the 1880s. By 1920, 70 per cent of the Black population lived in the Arkansas Delta region (Barnes, 2004). As Black progress and political activism continued, Black farmers and civic, religious, and business organizations continued to spread the word about opportunities in Arkansas.

These messages of hope and political and economic opportunity were heard in Friars Point, and Lizzie and her family were persuaded to go to Helena, Arkansas. Willie Ann explained why they moved to Helena, saying to Robertson, "How did I come here? When I was 14, my family heard how fine this State [Arkansas] was and moved to Helena [Phillips County]. I also lived at Moro [Lee County] and Cotton Plant [Woodruff County]." In 1888, poor Black and White farmers began forging agrarian coalitions, leading to a biracial rural agrarian movement with economic benefits and political power. By 1890, Black people in Phillips, Lee, and Woodruff Counties were 75 per cent of the population (Barnes, 2004; Gordon, 1993). By 1891, the Black rural and urban middle-class political electorate was growing and gaining power with increasingly more Black elected officials in the Arkansas Delta, threatening the white political structure that had been in place for years. The response to black progress was white rage (Anderson, 2016) in the form of physical attacks and lynchings, and legislative violence through the legalization and institutionalization of Jim Crow in the state from 1880 to 1968, laying the foundation for race relations that continue today in the state (Gordon, 1993).

The Jim Crow South part I

"When the Arkansas General Assembly authored disfranchise-ment and Jim Crow segregation laws in early 1891, [the] interest in emigration became, in the words of Black Arkansas, 'Liberia fever,'" writes Barnes (2004, p. 49). The institution of Jim Crow laws and increasing white terrorism in Arkansas continued to strip away at the political and economic gains and independence Black people accomplished, spurring a back-to-Africa movement to Liberia in the late 1800s in Arkansas. Barnes (2004) offered that although the idea of migrating back to Africa had never died, the idea seemed to ebb and flow in Arkansas with shifts in Black Americans' political and economic conditions. Barnes (2004, p. 48) explained, "It was the failure of biracial agrarian populism beginning with the elections of 1888 that re-ignited the African emigration movement in a general way throughout the state."

Lizzie and her family were among those wanting to leave the state and country after having their dreams for a better life in Arkansas dashed. Willie Ann explained to Robertson how her family ended up in Brinkley, as they realized that Arkansas was not "the fine state" they had heard about when living in Friars Point.

> The way I came here was funny. A man came up there [Helena] and said there is a free train that will take us back to Africa. All who wanted to go could go. My pa sold about all that we had, and we came here [Brinkley] like they said. No train has come yet going to Africa.

She continued,

> My pa gave that white man $5.00 to pay for the train. Tom Watson was one of them, too. He was sort of the leader among those wanting to go back. Well, when the day came for that train to arrive, everyone came to the depot where the train was going to stop. There was a big crowd. Yes, ma'am, we dressed up and had little provisions and clothes fixed up. We stayed around here a week or two, waiting to hear something or to be ready to go. Most everyone stayed pretty close to the depot for two or three days. Yes, ma'am, there sure was a crowd— a whole big train full from here and other places. The depot agent told us he didn't know about a train going to Africa. The tickets were no good on his train.

Like many other Black families desperate to escape the white racial violence and control surrounding their lives, Lizzie's family had become vulnerable targets of imposters posing as agents of the formal organizations that assisted families interested in emigrating to Liberia. The impostors would travel around Arkansas fraudulently collecting money from Black families and making unfulfilled promises to help them get to Liberia (Barnes, 2004). Families camping around train stations for weeks were also sub-jected to harassment to disband by White sheriffs. Black people wanting to leave were also at risk of being lynched by White mobs trying to curtail their travel to maintain racial and eco-nomic control over their lives and labor.

Once in Brinkley, Willie Ann decided to stay. She married and, with her husband, bought land and raised a family with three children: two daughters, Ida and Lizzie "L.C.," and a son, Sherman. The family made a way out of no way by farming, working mul-tiple jobs, and selling goods from Willie Ann's garden. Willie Ann told Robertson:

> I just stayed here [Brinkley], and I've been here ever since. How do I own this place? I'll tell you. A man here had all this land around here laid off. He couldn't sell any of his lots. They wouldn't buy his lots. So, he came to me. We made a good crop, so I got up the money and bought this place. One hundred dollars is what I gave him. Others then started settling in around close to my place.

She continued explaining how she and her husband supported themselves. "The way I am supported is my husband gets all the jobs he is able to do and can, and the government gives us $10 a month. We also have a little garden."

Raising their children in a racially hostile environment required expediency. For Willie Ann, this meant being clear and direct. She explained to Irene, "When my children come, I tell them you are grown, and you know right from wrong. Do right. That's all

I know to say."Willie Ann lived in the rural community 2 miles east of Brinkley for 68 years until she died of malaria on August 24, 1959. She was 91 years old. Her oldest daughter, Ida, my great-grandmother, was born in 1880, shortly after the family arrived in Helena, Arkansas.

By 1900, Ida married Dennis Hall and had one child, Eleanor. The family lived in Wheatley, Arkansas, with Dennis' mother, Anna Sayers, who was also from Arkansas, two of his sisters, two brothers, and a cousin—ranging in age from 4 to 13 years old, according to the 1900 census. The census listed Dennis as 24 years old and Ida as 20 years old. Between 1899 and 1924, Dennis and Ida Henderson Hall had 12 more children—Elverta, Essie, Ollie, James, Gussie, Booker, Oliver, Huester, Jannie, Berdine (my grandmother), J.D., and Rayford. The 1880 census, as well as death certificates, confirm that Dennis' family lived in Arkansas. His father, Monroe Hall, born in Arkansas in 1858, and mother, Anna Sayers, born in Arkansas in 1859, are recorded in the 1880 census as 22 and 21 years old, respectively, living with their two children, Dennis, 7 years old, and his 2-year-old sister, Lucy. In the 1880 census, Monroe's occupation is recorded as "Farmer" and Anna's as "Keeping house."

Jim Crow South part II

The first time I formally interviewed my grandmother, I was a 17-year-old business major in an undergraduate class on entrepreneurship at the University of Nebraska-Omaha. The major assignment in the class was to interview five entrepreneurs throughout the semester and find out what makes them tick. So, Grandma was my first formal oral history interview. Little did

I know then that I would interview her many more times throughout her life. She was always on the go, and I trailed behind her with my tape recorder, earnestly trying to fulfill my assignment. She moved around the house, finishing the housework before preparing to work at her business, a ten-minute drive away, the Williams Care Manor, where she was the director of nurses. Between folding clothes, doing the dishes, sweeping the floor, and rearranging and dusting furniture, she reflected on her life, sharing bits and pieces with me when it suited her timing and the rhythms of her work.

She told me she was inspired to become a doctor after traveling around her rural community as a child with her grandmother, Willie Ann, who cared for the sick and helped deliver babies. Describing Willie Ann as a "mid-wife and healer who helped both Black and White families," she paused her work, looked at me directly with her high cheekbones and piercing warm brown eyes, and said, "We come from a long line of healers." Then, returning to her task, she shared, almost like an afterthought, "Those White folks respected my grandma just as much as the Black ones did."

Racial violence, sharecropping, and domestic work

My grandparents were born in rural Arkansas in 1919, roughly 60 miles from the site of the 1919 Elaine Massacre (Stockley, n.d.) in Phillips County, in the adjacent cities of Wheatley and Marianna. The Encyclopedia of Arkansas (2024) framed the massacre like this, "While its deepest roots lay in the state's commitment to white supremacy, the events in and around Elaine

[Phillips County] stemmed from tense race relations and growing concerns about labor unions" (n.p.). Black farmers continued to organize coalitions to challenge a "sharecropping system that had degenerated into peonage" (Gordon, 1993, p. 127). They gathered at a church on the evening of September 30, 1919, to consider unionizing to demand a fair price for their cotton crops from the White plantation landowners after years of exploitation and domination during the era of Jim Crow.

A descendant of a Black family that survived the massacre reported that White landowners were selling their cotton for 50 cents a pound but only paying Black farmers 1 cent per pound for the cotton crops they bought from them. Threatened by the potential loss of revenue and White domination over the Black farming community, an armed White posse, a large mob of White people from Elaine and surrounding areas, and federal troops went on a four-day killing spree. They murdered nearly 100 Black men, women, and children and arrested close to 300 Black people. Five White people also lost their lives, according to the Encyclopedia of Arkansas (2024).

Descendants of Black families that survived the massacre put the number of Black lives lost in the thousands and say that White people initiated the killing to steal land from Black farmers facilitated by the local White authorities that allowed them to change the names of Black farmers recorded on land deeds at the time of the killings.

At the time of the massacre, my great-grandparents, Dennis and Ida Hall, already had five boys and five girls between the ages of 3 and 20. My grandmother was 6 months old, and Grandpa was born 15 days after the attacks and murders. It is not difficult to imagine the terror and grief that undoubtedly engulfed my great-grandparents and other Black families, eclipsing their joy in welcoming a newborn while doing everything within their power to protect themselves and their children from the racial violence surrounding them.

The children of sharecroppers, my grandparents, were born into and essentially lived the first 25 years of their lives navigating the racial violence of the same white power structure during the Jim Crow era that their grandparents had previously during the period of Reconstruction in the South. Their lives were regularly threatened by Klan violence, random violence of any kind, and the inhumanity of being restricted by segregationist laws and customs that dictated where they could live, walk, attend school, worship, work, and socialize. They learned from their elders and older siblings how and when to resist, ignore, and abide by the racial codes imposed on their daily lives.

Grandma grew up like her siblings, working on their family farm. The sharecropping system in the South is often described as slavery by another name. Instituted by White plantation owners during reconstruction after the Civil War, it allowed White land-owners to reestablish a labor force by economically exploiting newly freed Black families. Unfortunately, many formerly enslaved families typically did not own their land and homes after slavery. They were forced to work as tenant farmers on the land of their previous enslavers, usually with unfavorable contracts that kept them in debt bondage and poverty for generations. Instead of paying the landowner cash, the landowners took a portion of the crop yield from the farmers as payment for land use.

In addition to sharecropping, my great-grandmother Ida worked as a domestic worker, cleaning the houses and doing the laundry of White families. At the age of ten years old, Grandma started going to work with her mother to care for the children in some of those homes. Blistering heat and humidity continually threatened Grandma's health, keeping her out of the cotton fields. She explained, "Because of my asthma, I couldn't pick cotton like my brothers and sisters, but sometimes I carried water to them when they were in the fields." Everybody in the family helped in whatever way they could. For example, Grandma shared,

> My momma had this great big garden, and she raised guineas; well, she got those guineas by my brother James becoming a musician. He played piano for little places in Arkansas, and this woman didn't have any money to pay him, so she gave him a set of guineas. So that's how my momma started raising guineas because of my brother.

Of her five older brothers, Booker was Grandma's favorite. "He taught me how to help on the farm, care for the house, and encouraged me to do well in school." Her brother Oliver was her least favorite. She recalled, "He didn't want to work on the family farm, but he sure would work for the White folks to make his own money."

The WPA and education

In the late 1930s, during the Depression, Franklin D. Roosevelt created the Works Progress Administration (WPA) as part of his New Deal policy to address the growing unemployed population and lift the country out of the Great Depression. Grandma said her father "laid his crop aside to go out on jobs working for the WPA." Dennis made enough money working for the WPA to pay for Grandma and one of her brothers to attend school. A conscientious and determined student, Grandma loved learning. She reflected on her education with pride and joy, sharing,

> Let me tell you who my teachers were. I had Neale McGettis. She was my music teacher. I had Ruth Branch Comb and Professor Hayes. My economics teacher was Theresa Warren. She looked just like she was White, oh, but she was so sweet. They all were sweet, but Theresa Warren was very sweet. She put me in a play. I got married in this play, and she let me wear the wedding gown that she got married in. Honey! I tell you, I used to be a very, very good scholar.

In grade school, one of Grandma's favorite classes was spelling. "I was the spelling champ," she said, beaming with delight. She recalled, "My name was in the *Brinkley Gazette* and the *Brinkley Democrat* every week." Then eager, she hastily asked, "Do you know what the word was? I never will forget it … 'afraid!' couldn't nobody spell 'afraid!'" Grinning like a Cheshire cat now, Grandma remembered how she spelled it and told us, "I said 'Afraid,' and I spelled it 'A-F-R-A-I-D' and then I said it again 'Afraid' because you have to say the word before and after you spell it or it won't count," she clarified. Then, as her voice rose to a crescendo, she declared, "My teacher said, 'Come on up here, Hall, I knew you could do it!'" Grandma was also proud of one of her older sisters, Jannie, who attended Shorter College, a private historically Black junior college in Little Rock, Arkansas, founded in 1886 by the African Methodist Episcopal (AME) Church.

When she was not in school or caring for little White children, Grandma enjoyed traveling around the community with her grandmother, Willie Ann, helping her visit the sick and deliver babies. She was receiving the hands-on education and skills she needed to prepare her for a career one day in nursing and the eventual opening of her residential care center. She cultivated her dream with every visit she went on with her grandmother.

Land purchase

In 1944, over four decades after their marriage and two years after my great-grandfather Dennis died, Ida saved enough money to purchase 17.1 acres of land from an African American couple, Homer P. Lampkin and his wife Cornelia Lampkin, for $513.00 cash in hand—in Monroe County, Arkansas. Ida bought the land on October 27, 1944. The deed reads, "We hereby grant, sell, and convey unto the said Ida Hall and unto her heirs and assigns forever, the following lands lying in Monroe and State of Arkansas."

Less than two months later, on December 16, 1944, Ida created her will, first appointing her daughter Jannie McMillan "as executrix of this my last will and testament and request that she be allowed to serve without bond." Second, Ida directed "that my said executrix, as soon as practicable after my death, pay all my just debts and funeral expenses." Third, Ida "will[ed] and bequeath[ed] all personal property of which I may die seized and all my real estate consisting of the following described land in Monroe County Arkansas, to wit: [dimensions of the land] to my children and grandchildren share and share alike." She named each of her children and her grandson and described the land's dimensions as described in the deed. The land remains in the family. On her 98th birthday in 2017, Grandma, the last surviving child of Dennis and Ida, bequeathed the land to her granddaughter, my sister, Jendayi. Ida Henderson Hall died in 1961 at 80 years old in St Louis, Missouri.

As historian Carole Emberton notes in her essay, "'Cleaning Up the Mess': Some thoughts on freedom, violence, and grief" (2017), for Black survivors of the violence of slavery, civil war, reconstruction, Black codes, and Jim Crow, land ownership is often more than a symbol of economic independence. It can also be a physical and spiritual space that links the past and present and serves as a means of remembering and honoring one's ancestors and the sacrifices they endured, paving the way for their present and future generations of kin. Our land serves as a geographical memorial of our family lineage.

Marriage and migration

According to their marriage certificate, Bobby and Berdine married in 1943 in Little Rock, Arkansas. Grandpa was working for the railroad in Arkansas as a cook, and a representative of Swift & Company was on the train one day and liked how Grandpa cut and prepared his steak. He told Grandpa that if he could get to Omaha, he would have a job there waiting for him.

Like many other Black families leaving the South during the second great migration, my grandparents were looking for a better way of life with more economic, political, and social freedom and an opportunity for their children to get a good education. But I can only imagine how difficult it must have been to leave one of the "prized" positions White people allowed for Black employment on the promise of a White man, a stranger at that, and a requirement to move to an unfamiliar place hundreds of miles away from home. But leave is what they did. With their two children, Ida (my mother), age four, and one-year-old Bobbie Jean, Bobby and Berdine moved from Little Rock, Arkansas, to Omaha, Nebraska, on a promise and a prayer.

When they arrived in South Omaha, the rep. of Swift & Co. honored his promise. Grandpa became a butcher for Swift Packing Plant, a division of Swift & Co., and my grandmother found work in hospitals. Housing discrimination in Omaha resulted in my grandparents living in the garage of a Jewish family on the south side of Omaha with their children until Mr. Locket, an African American man who worked with my grandpa, helped them find housing on the north side of Omaha in the predominately Black part of the city. They had two more children, Doris, born in 1945, and Kinze, born in 1947. They bought their first house on the north side in 1948 at 2608 Blondo Street, four years after they arrived in Omaha. It was a couple blocks west of 24th Street. Their neighbors helped them acclimate to the city, culture, and neighborhood. Faith was a big part of the way my grandparents coped with prejudice. They found a church home in Mount Moriah Missionary Baptist Church, a historic Black church in North Omaha, and remained faithful members for 75 years. Grandpa was a Deacon and Grandma a Deaconess; she also served on the nursing board. The Smiths, the neighbors across the street, helped care for their children, taking them to Sunday school when my grandparents had to work on weekends. They lived in the Blondo Street house for another four years before purchasing a white two-story, five-bedroom home at 2801 Pratt Street in 1952. Both homes were on the Near North Side of Omaha.

Chapter 2
History of
North Omaha

I loved hearing rubber tires rolling along the cobblestone streets when cars passed through our 28th & Pratt Street neighborhood. The sound reminded me of bowling balls rolling down the lane before they hit the pins. A constant low-pitched rumble signaled a familiar knowing that my body and soul were at home, safely cocooned in a space that recognized and nurtured me without pause. Growing up in a segregated Black working-class neighborhood in North Omaha meant I could take certain things for granted.

Most of our neighbors and those living within a certain radius looked like me racially. I could take for granted that when I walked to Kelly's Drugstore to buy pork skins, penny candy, and dill pickles in a bag, there would be plenty of them, and the person behind the counter waiting on me would most likely be Black. I could take for granted that if I deviated from my route home from the drugstore and ventured onto a street I had no business on, my grandparents would know about it before I made it home. I could take for granted that Larry, the Black man who owned our neighborhood grocery store, Larry's Station, would stock his meat department with neckbones, chicken gizzards, and chitlins and have a variety of greens—collard, turnip, and mustard—all year round. I could count on reading about community events in *The Omaha Star*, Nebraska's only Black-owned newspaper. I did not have to wait until Black History Month to learn about civic engagement, the achievements of Black leaders, or significant community traditions. Instead, I could witness, participate in, and read about them regularly.

Living in North Omaha meant that, during the week, neighbors would be busily focused on getting to and from work. On the weekends, the rhythm of the neighborhood would slow down, with folk lingering on their porches and front stoops to greet one another, swap stories, and gossip. I could see and hear the roar of lawnmowers and the swishing of brooms sweeping sidewalks in front of houses leading up to porches. I would see backs bent over in the dirt, tending to gardens or in driveways washing cars. And arms stretched high in the air, hanging up or taking down fresh laundry, flapping in the breeze on makeshift clotheslines. I could count on the rain to wash away the hop-scotch game we scratched on the sidewalk with just the perfect rock. I could count on playing Double Dutch with Jendayi, cousin Tracy, and our friends Susie and Barbara, who lived across the street, or watching pick-up basketball in the empty dirt lot where a house once stood.

I could take for granted that, on Sundays, neighbors dressed to the nines would leave their homes mid-morning, heading off to various worship houses with names that included A.M.E., Baptist, Methodist, and Zion. And I could count on the aromas of backyard barbeques and fish fries permeating the air, mingling with the heat and humidity and the zest of potato salad, watermelon, homemade ice cream, and sock-it-to-me cake saturating my taste buds all summer long. Finally, I could take for granted that many of my teachers would be Black. We would pledge allegiance to the United States of America every day in school, but as a 4th grader at Franklin Elementary, we would also "Lift Every Voice and Sing" "till earth and heaven ring … with the harmonies of Liberty …[and] march on till victory is won." It would be many years into my adulthood before I truly understood the full meaning of that hymn, dubbed the Black national anthem, written by James Weldon Johnson and set to music by his brother J. Rosamond Johnson in 1900.

Black human geography encompasses sites, activities, and events that assert the fundamental social value of Black people, transforming how urban space is understood, shaped, and experienced (Carter, 2014). The story of North Omaha is inextricably linked to a history and social geography of confinement and racial and class oppression, and simultaneously a long legacy of spiritual and civic community building and social and economic engagement. The city's demography must be understood within the more extensive, complicated intersections of race and class history and how Black people navigated, created, and claimed space to assert their humanity, create spatial inclusion, and mobilize to fight for equity and justice.

Redlining

When my grandparents moved to Omaha in 1944, they did not know that the city shared a history of racial strife with the South that would lay the foundation for the prejudice and discrimination they would have to navigate almost immediately upon their arrival. They moved from the segregated South to the segregated North. Omaha, the largest city in Nebraska, was founded along the Missouri River in 1854, while North Omaha's roots date back to 1812. The racial lines that divided Omaha were etched in stone early in the nineteenth century when White people confined African Americans to "the north side Negro district [that] extends for several blocks on 24th St." (FWP, 1939, p. 222).

North 24th Street was in an area with a remarkable commercial heritage dating back to the late 1870s. The place had a rich history of Eastern European immigrant, Jewish, and African American business enterprises and culture spanning six decades from the 1870s through the 1930s. "The North 24th St. area became its own 'Black Wall Street,' bustling with Black-owned newspapers, doctors' offices, lawyers, social clubs, churches, and other establishments" (Vireo, 2021, p. 7). Black people on the Near North Side demonstrated through their daily experiences how Black urban bodies transpose spatial limitations and create embodied geographies and narratives that value, embrace, and advance Black self-determination, empowerment, and success. There was a Black YWCA, Black Red Cross nurses, Black schools, funeral homes, and a nursing home by the early 1920s. Black families were beginning to flourish in North Omaha.

However, at the same time, this enterprising, ethnically diverse Northside community was spatially bound by race-restrictive covenants enforced by White landlords, real estate operations, and White property owners. Redlining, predatory lending practices, and other tactics used by federally backed financial and insurance corporations restricted and confined Black economic, social, and political progress. Practices of widespread structural racism made it impossible for Black land and homeowners to maintain their property adequately. White city planners also deliberately withdrew services to the area (Vireo, 2021). These collective white supremacist forces combined with decades of police brutality, race riots, and natural and economic disasters, like tornados and the great depression, disproportionately impacted working-class and Black families and neighborhoods in North Omaha and resulted in urban blight and white flight over the next 80 years. When my grandparents moved to North Omaha, it had become a primarily Black neighborhood.

As the award-winning journalist and creator of *The 1619 Project,* Nikole Hannah-Jones observed in writing about justice and the Fair Housing Act, "racial segregation in the North had largely been accomplished through housing discrimination" (2021, p. 454). The same New Deal program that provided my great-grandpa Dennis Hall with the opportunity to lay down his crop and work for the WPA in Arkansas would deny my grandparents and millions of other Black families access to federally back mortgages from 1934 to 1962 when the New Deal's Federal Housing Administration (FHA) program used red ink to redline maps, to mark neighborhoods where Black people lived to signal that they were uninsurable. The Federal Housing Act was passed in 1968, barring housing discrimination based on race, gender, disability, and other identity categories. Still, it would not come soon enough to benefit my grandparents, and it would not stop White financial and real estate institutions from using other tactics to maintain racial segregation.

One of the only viable options available for Black families to build better homes and gain economic security for themselves was the establishment, in 1944, of the first Black-owned financial institution, Carver Savings and Loan Association, founded by a movement of Black leaders organized by North Omaha attorneys Charles F. Davis and Dr Craig Morris. It opened its doors for service in 1946 at 2416 Lake Street to provide a means for Black families on the Near North Side to secure residential loans. It operated for 20 years until 1965 (Carter Legacy Center, n.d.). It is said to have provided more loans to Black families to buy homes within three years than any White financial institution did in the previous decade (Sanchez, 2021). Despite gaining access to mortgages, racist segregationist practices continued to restrict Black homeownership and mobility primarily to North Omaha.

From garage to house

"It had a rug on the floor and a toilet," Aunt Doris remembered. She said they rented the car garage from a Jewish lady. Her name was Yael. Mom would rather forget it. She does not want anyone to know they lived in a garage in South Omaha. If she talked about it at all, it was with reluctance, and she described it as a "garage converted into an apartment." "Hmmm. So it had furniture and beds and a table and chairs?" I asked her. "I don't remember," she responded somewhat impatiently. Her embarrassment is understandable, although misplaced. I got the message, though, and did not press her further.

Instead, I took stock of it all. I thought about what it must have been like for my grandparents to have two children born at home in the South, where hospitals were segregated, and two children born in a hospital in the North, where housing segregation meant they had to live in a garage. Do these trade-offs represent "progress" or "a step up in the world"? Or a step up in a world hell-bent on keeping you down? They traveled hundreds of miles from a home in the South to make a garage into a home in the North. I was well into adulthood before Grandma told me she and Grandpa lived in a garage when they came to Omaha. She did not say it was a garage converted into an apartment. She said, "You make do with what you have until you can do better, Lord willing."

As a young family starting in a new city, I can imagine that my grandparents were gripped by joy, excitement, anxiety, and fear as they learned to navigate the racialized landscape of their new environment. They would have to decode the race, class, and gender signposts that generations before them also had to learn to survive and thrive in the North. Living through four seasons of harsh Omaha winters in a garage with their children, they held on to each other and many of their Southern traditions for comfort and to provide for themselves, and they reached out for support.

My grandparents moved right in the middle of an area known as "The Black Box." Geographically, the boundaries of the Black Box extended roughly one square mile from Locust and Cuming Streets from north to the south and North 20th to 30th Streets to the east and west. Black families and businesses were confined to the Black Box, and by 1936, this covert practice of housing discrimination became more explicit when the Federal Home Owners Lending Corporation, in conjunction with Omaha's real estate and banking industries, drew a red line around the area on a map and systematically denied residential and commercial loans to Black people attempting to secure them or move outside of the racially segregated zone.

The Blondo Street house had two bedrooms. Aunt Bobby Jean, Aunt Doris, and Uncle Kenzie shared a bedroom, and Ida, my mom, slept on a roll-away bed in the kitchen. "It was like having my own space at night for the first time," Mom recalled. They traded in concrete walls for a home with windows that allowed golden sunrays to light up rugs now covering wooden floors instead of concrete when the curtains were open. Excitedly, Aunt Doris shared, "We had a screened-in front and back porch!" They went from having no backyard to a "big backyard where Daddy built play furniture for us. Sometimes, however, we played on the stairs of the Masonic Hall right around the corner a block away."

"A Jewish grocery store sat on the corner of Blondo and 24th Street, where everyone in the neighborhood bought groceries," Mom recalled fondly. "I went to Long Elementary School; it was in the neighborhood within walking distance," she said. "Daddy worked during the day, so he was home with us at night when Momma went to work at the hospital or nursing homes. She often worked double shifts, so sometimes I didn't see her until I came home from school the next day." Mrs. Margarite, the next-door neighbor, would babysit the children in the morning between the hours Grandpa had to leave for work and Grandma arrived home from her shift at the nursing home. She was also available in the afternoons to babysit. Mom explained,

> If Momma worked a double shift, we knew to go over
> to Mrs. Margarite's house when we got home from
> school until Momma got home from work in the early

afternoon. Mrs. Margarite was a chain smoker, so her house reeked of smoke all the time, and Momma made us leave our smoke-filled clothes on the porch before we entered the house after we stayed at Mrs. Margarite's.

The Smiths' legacy

Shortly after my grandparents moved to the Blondo Street house, an older African American couple, Paul and Harriet Smith, helped them navigate their new neighborhood and surrounding areas. The Smiths lived across the street in a big green two-story corner house trimmed in white and surrounded by a wrap-around porch and a big, luscious yard. Their home looked like it took up a fourth of the block and could easily hold 10 or 15 children, but the Smiths had no children. The houses near theirs paled in comparison. The Smiths lived alone in that big house, but they let Grandpa use their backyard to make a garden. They became the godparents to my mother and her siblings, letting them pick fruit from the pear tree in their yard and taking them to Mount Moriah Missionary Baptist Church with them on Sundays. They essentially "adopted" my grandparents and their children, seeing them as a young family from the South needing support and guidance on how to live in the North.

The Smiths' generosity and influence extended beyond their lives. Before their death, they willed their house to my grandparents and the furniture inside to their godchildren. By the time they died, my grandparents had already purchased their five-bedroom home on Pratt Street, which they had converted into a residential care center. The Smiths' home became the perfect place to stay during my childhood when my family visited

Omaha. We stayed in the "Green House," which my siblings and I called it to distinguish it from the Pratt Street house when my whole family visited my grandparents. There were six of us, two adults and four children, and the Green House provided plenty of room. If the family visited my grandparents during the summer, they would stay for a few weeks, but I stayed the whole summer. After the family left, I would stay at the Pratt Street house with my grandparents.

The furniture inside the Green House was made of mahogany and just as big and grand as the house it sat inside. Massive brown chairs of heavy wood with red velvet seat cushions and high, sturdy backs towered behind our heads as children when we sat in them, feet dangling above the floor. Two chairs at either end of the dining table had fancy armrests and elaborate designs on the back. They were built for royalty, I thought as a child. The chairs with armrests were designated for adults. Only my parents sat in them.

The dining room table was long, heavy, and wide, even without the leaf that fits in its middle to extend it more, making my parents look miles apart, seated at each end of the table when our family sat down for dinner. The dining room set somehow formalized our eating rituals in that room, quietly commanding structure, attentive deference, and grace from us towards each other. It required us to practice the manners we were raised with and set the order of the house. We all knew our place, who would sit where when we entered the grand dining room for dinner. The elegant crystal chandelier hanging from the ceiling signaled a space of refinement that added charm and formality. We could play in the kitchen adjacent to the dining room, separated by a wall with a single door. We could play in the living room on the other side of the dining room, an open archway trimmed in dark brown wooden beams and frames that marked a division between the rooms, as did the change in furniture. But we could never play in the dining room, and we had to walk through it, not run, to get to the kitchen or living room. An imposing buffet matched the dining room table and chairs, hugging most of the wall shared by the kitchen. It was a magnificent treasure with elaborately designed brass handles featured prominently in the middle of each of its drawers, except for the secret drawer at the top that just looked like an ordinary panel. It could only be accessed by pulling open the drawer below it first and then reaching up under it with your hand, palm side up, to grab the slither of a lip below it to pull it out. We only found out the secret drawer existed when we were adults. Hence, the name we called it after my mother took possession of the dining room set, and it was moved to our house many years later.

We could open the drawers of the buffet only to retrieve the tablecloth and matching placemats, cloth napkins, and silverware to adorn the table before dinner during our summer visits. This ritual of setting the table added to the splendor and formality of the space. A beautiful beige marble-top end table with exquisitely designed S-shaped sturdy wooden legs rounded out the furniture in the dining room. The rest of the house furnishings seemed rather ordinary in comparison. When we stayed in the Green House, we helped Grandpa harvest his garden, played on the huge porch, and picked fruit from the trees. We were the third generation to benefit from the legacy of Paul and Harriet Smith.

The boning knife

Swift Packing Plant, a division of Swift & Co. located in South Omaha, had been slaughtering cattle and hogs for over a half-century when Grandpa started working there in 1944. The company opened its doors in 1887, and by the twentieth century it had gained international prominence for its stockyards and meatpacking plants. As a result, it was known as one of the "Big Four" meatpacking companies in the industry. Grandpa worked there for 25 years, becoming a head butcher, until the plant was closed in 1969. When Swift closed its Omaha division, they wanted Grandpa to relocate to Colorado, but he did not want to uproot his family again, so he retired.

Grandpa worked at the packing house for the first nine years of my life. The Grandpa I grew up with, however, was an entrepreneur and set his work hours, typically from sunup to sundown. He wore overalls most of the time, except Sundays when he donned a suit and tie for church. In contrast, as a butcher for Swift, Aunt Doris recalled, "he worked from nine to five every day but did not bring work worries home when he arrived in the evenings just in time for dinner." She fondly reminisced about him "getting down on hands and knees, giving us horsey-back rides around the house, playing catch in the backyard, and leaving the discipline, mostly up to momma."

Some of the "work worries" Grandpa left at his doorstep undoubtedly revolved around race relations within the plant and the city itself. Most White meatpacking workers lived in South Omaha near the meatpacking plants, while most Black workers were segregated in North Omaha. Segregated work and living conditions added to racial tensions in Omaha. Tensions between White and Black workers in Omaha prevailed into the 1930s and continued throughout the 1960s. Simultaneously, during the same time, unionization in the meatpacking industry took hold after several failed attempts in the early twentieth century. Like their working-class White counterparts, Black packinghouse workers participated in unionization efforts during the 1930s and 1940s to fight for better wages and work conditions, but additionally, union involvement aided them in their efforts toward racial equity and civil rights to some degree (Horowitz, 1997).

The packing plant industry was notorious for hazardous work conditions, low wages, and poor management and employee relations—conditions that resulted in many worker strikes. After decades of union-busting tactics and failures by earlier unions, the Congress of Industrial Organizations (CIO) chartered the Packinghouse Workers Organizing Committee (PWOC) in 1937, and by 1943 the PWOC was officially chartered as the United Packinghouse Workers of America (UPWA). In addition to fighting for higher wages and better work conditions, the UPWA was committed to interracial cooperation and created an Anti-Discrimination department devoted to ending racial discrimination in meat packing plants and working against segregation in local communities (Horowitz, 1997). The success of the UPWA in addressing racial discrimination varied based on the unique race relations that dominated local communities. Racism in Omaha shaped the effectiveness of the UPWA's anti-discrimination goals. Despite challenges, African American meatpacking workers in Omaha helped create the racially integrated United Meatpacking Workers of America union, ending segregated jobs in the industry and supporting the integration of public facilities in the 1950s.

UPWA workers nationwide went on strike in 1948, including in Omaha. The strike lasted over seven weeks, and workers demanded a wage increase of 29 cents an hour but offered to accept a 19-cent increase, countering the 9-cent raise proposed by the "Big Four" packing companies (Warren, 1996). "Momma was worried, but Daddy reassured her weekly that the family would be okay," said Aunt Doris, as she recalled Grandpa joining the strike. He was out of work for almost three months. Grandma was doing private nursing work then, but not enough to make ends meet, so she wanted to work more. They lived off their savings mostly during the strike and what Grandma made as a private nurse working in nursing homes, hospitals, and the homes of White folk. Grandpa returned to work with more pay but the same hazardous work conditions.

Many years after the packing plant closed, a member of Mount Moriah who worked as a young man at Swift & Co. during the day and went to school at night recalled with gratitude and appreciation that, "Every day, I would come to work in the morning and find that Mr. Bobby had cleaned my work boots right along with his own. His kindness helped me get to school on time after work and made a difference in me finishing my degree." Grandpa's small gesture of support had a lasting impact.

Besides the skill with which Grandpa wielded a knife around the kitchen, the visceral and physical evidence I have of him as a skilled butcher is the sharp homemade six-inch boning knife he gave me when I was separating from my former husband and had to go to our apartment to pack my things and leave. The thin, curved, tarnished blade attached to the worn and stained brown handle held together with nails looked like something from an ancient time. Grandpa told me, "Don't hesitate to use it." I did not know then, but he did, that the thin blade prevents drag through meat, and the curve makes it easier to get into joints and right along bones. I stuck the knife in my backpack, blade first, so I could grab that ancient-looking tool by the handle if I needed it. I am grateful that I did not.

Grandpa also gave me a worn grey whetstone with a tiny chip on the edge of its smooth side, the other rougher. He showed me how to keep my boning knife sharp by gracefully gliding the blade along the stone with slow, smooth, even strokes, like gently rocking a baby back and forth. It was a hypnotizing motion to watch and signaled that his hands knew their way around a blade without hesitation. I wondered what I would have experienced had I had to pull that knife from my backpack that day I moved out of my apartment and back with my grandparents.

Many years later, having given up on my ability to use the whetstone with the skill my grandpa demonstrated, I took the knife to a store to have it sharpened. The older man behind the counter who waited on me commented, "Whoever made this knife knew what they were doing. I don't see too many knives like this anymore," as he proceeded to show me how the handle was constructed to sandwich the blade neatly between the worn wood on each side of the blade. I proudly told him, "My grandfather gave it to me," leaving out the details surrounding the circumstances of the gift. As part of our upbringing, Grandpa used to tell us that "a dull knife is more dangerous than a sharp one in the hands of someone who doesn't know how to use a knife." Since he did most of the cooking, especially the meats we ate, I watched Grandpa cut and slice with purpose and precision for most of my life. Perhaps this gave him and me the confidence I needed when he handed me the boning knife.

Is there room for me?

Grandma wanted to go to Prospect Hill Cemetery to visit Grandpa's grave site one day. He died in 1994, 26 years ahead of her. By this time, she was 100 years old and occasionally used a wheelchair, having had surgery for a fractured hip from a fall when she was 99. I wheeled her in front of Grandpa's headstone, located between an unknown marker to the left and Mathilda E. Yaeger, the first wife of Barney E. Yaeger, on the right. Barney's headstone was on the other side of Mathilda's, followed by the gravestone of his second wife, Alice M. Yaeger. Next to Alice was the tombstone of Grandpa's brother, my great-uncle Nelson. We stood there for several minutes in silence as we paid our respects. Then, in a soft, barely audible whisper, Grandma asked, "Is there room for me?" as she looked up at me, her face pleading. I knew as well as she could see that there was no way she could be interred next to her husband when she died, but I lied and said, "Yes, Grandma, there is room for you." She had to be buried in front of Grandpa when she died, and almost every time I visit their grave sites, I am reminded of that day. Even in death, the White people Grandma cared for as a private duty nurse have a way of interfering with the intimate spaces of our family life.

Grandma worked as a nurse for the Yaeger family for over 15 years, caring for Mathilda, Barney, and eventually Alice, who was the Yaeger family's housekeeper for many years until Mathilda died. Barney was planning to deed Grandma a portion of his estate in gratitude for her care for so many years. The family lawyer encouraged Barney to marry Alice instead so she would become the sole inheritor of his estate. Aunt Doris explained,

> Barney's lawyer didn't want him giving his money to a Black woman, so he kept telling Barney to marry Alice so she could get his estate after he died. Barney resisted for a while but eventually caved in and married Alice, hoping she would ensure that Momma would be given a share of his estate. Alice did not follow her promise to share some of the family's money with Momma.

Grandma had nursed Barney back to health so he could walk again and drive after a stroke. Before he died, Barney purchased the cemetery plots at Prospect Hill for himself, his two wives, and Grandma and Grandpa. Later, Grandma and Grandpa bought two more plots for Aunt Doris and Uncle Nelson. Aunt Doris remembered going to the Yaegers' house with Grandma when she went there to care for Alice, and one day, when they drove into the driveway, a young White couple from next door approached their car and told Grandma, "You are not welcome here anymore." Aunt Doris continued, "The couple took Alice to Kansas City, and the next time Momma heard from her, Alice was in a nursing home with an amputated leg from diabetes." Alice died in Kansas City, and her body was brought back to Omaha to be interred in Prospect Hill Cemetery.

As I stood with Grandma, remembering Grandpa, I measured how long she spent away from her family to care for the Yaegers by the date marking their deaths at the gravesite. Mathilda died in 1961, and Barney died in 1970, but whoever was responsible for Alice when her body was returned to Omaha for burial did not bother to put the year of her death on her gravestone. I imagined the quality of Grandma's interactions with the Yaegers by the date marking their births at the gravesite. Mathilda was born in 1886. Barney was born in 1887, and Alice was born in 1895. I wondered how White people born and raised during the Jim Crow era would have interacted with my grandmother as she cared for them. Prospect Hill Cemetery was founded in 1858 and is one of Nebraska's oldest cemeteries and a state historic site. My grandpa and great-uncle Nelson used to cut the grass at Prospect Hill Cemetery. At that time, I never imagined that they would one day be interred there along with my grandmother. It is a fitting resting place for them all.

The nursing industry

Black midwives and nurses were confronted by racism as the nursing industry moved toward professionalization. As they fought for integration and respect within the White nursing industry, many Black nurses worked long hours as private-duty or bedside nurses or in institutions and hospitals in intimate spaces with White folk (Hines, 1989). Black nurses were subjected to everyday individual and institutional racism and discrimination by White nurses, doctors, and patients. They were also subjected to long-standing stereotypes and roles of servitude that

Black people had been confined to for centuries. This meant that in White private home settings, they were exploited and expected to be submissive and deferential. In addition to caring for ill family members, they were also required to cook, clean, wash, and provide child care (Hines, 1989). This is why Grandma always wore her white nursing uniform, whether working in an institution or a private home, even after she started her residential care home. It was her internal and external symbol of respect for herself and her role as a nurse. It helped her project a professional identity, pride, and a strong self-image regardless of how the White doctors, nurses, and homeowners who hired her saw her role or what they expected of her as a Black woman.

Reminiscing about her nursing career at 100 years old, Grandma shared,

> I got away from those nursing homes. They work the life out of you but don't pay you what they are supposed to. Honey, I got away from that. I ran an ad in the paper to do private-duty nursing. I got so many calls I couldn't take them all! I took two of them. Honey, one woman wanted me to come from 7 am–3 pm. I told her I didn't know about that. I told her I have small kids and I have to see that they go to school. The other one wanted me to work an 11 pm–7 am shift. I told her I needed to talk to my husband about it on account of our kids. I worked it out so my kids could be taken care of, and after a week on that job, that woman gave me a raise! Do you hear me?!? Honey, she was rich and said she didn't care if I was black or white; all she wanted was a good nurse!

I stayed with them until they moved. I sure hated that they had to go. I was getting good pay, and then sometimes, they would give me a little extra pay. My husband said, "Honey, that woman is spoiling you," and I said, "I have to work for it too, and that's why she's spoiling me."

She laughed.

Honey, that's where I made my big money, working private duty, and I loved it. But sometimes, I would go to work at 7:00 in the morning, and I wouldn't see my husband and kids until 7:00 at night. Twelve hours, you hear me! Twelve hours, but I got paid for those twelve hours. I sit here now thinking about that, and I say, "One thing about me, God blessed me and my husband when we were younger, and He keeps on blessing us, that's right!"

Smiling contentedly, she testified, "I prayed for good jobs to help myself but also to help others. When God is in the plan, the devil can't do you no harm!" My mother recalled that during the polio epidemic,

Momma did a lot of private duty nursing, and dad didn't like her taking those cases because he didn't want her to bring that back to us children. Sometimes, she would stay at the family's home, come home on the weekend, and then return on Sunday night. At that time, she did make good money doing private duty nursing for families that were pretty well off, like doctors, lawyers, and professionals who had children with polio, mostly White families.

The Williams Care Manor

One of the lawyers my grandparents met through Grandma's private nursing work with wealthy White folk was Mr. Hayes. Mom remembered how helpful he was in completing the legal documents my grandparents needed to license and open their residential care center in 1954 at the 2801 Pratt St house. She said that "he was a good lawyer who helped people without much money. He was also very helpful to Mom and Dad in getting the other paperwork done to get the nursing home built at 3525 Evans Street in 1977." There were delays in building the Williams Care Manor, initially planned for construction in 1962 but delayed due to problems with financing and changes in state licenses and codes. Construction began in 1976 but was temporarily postponed due to vandalism. The Williams Care Manor opened its doors for business in October 1977. At capacity, the facility employed over 50 full-time and part-time employees, consultants, and physicians. It was described as "a leading example of minority business enterprise in the state" by William Moore, then executive director of the Urban Business Development Center in Omaha (*Omaha World-Herald*, 1979, p. 2).

Grandma and Grandpa received many public awards and recognition for their efforts to provide continuous healthcare in Nebraska. They were recognized with a proclamation from then-mayor Albert L. "Al" Veys in 1979. The Omaha City Council recognized them at the 30th anniversary of the Williams Care Manor, and they received a "Distinguished Community Service" award from the Charles Drew Health Center in Omaha for their contributions to healthcare in the community. A rededication ceremony was held in 1988 to install the cornerstone that was omitted when the building was erected. The cornerstone inscription, "Williams Care Manor. Established in 1954. Founded by Berdine Hall Williams. Dedicated to mankind," reflects Grandma's commitment and service.

As Grandma navigated many trials, tribulations, and triumphs, she remained steadfast in her focus on what she believed was a calling—caring for older adults. The long work hours, betrayals, disappointments, and setbacks did not deter her; instead, they fueled her passion, determination, and successes to realize her dream of becoming a nurse and opening the Williams Residential Care Home and later the Williams Care Manor.

PART II
Community pillars

Chapter 3
The Williams Residential Care Home

Berdine Williams at her house on Blondo Street

When I entered the Pratt Street house, it was like walking into an intricate maze with special rules and clues for moving around. The order, routine, and particular timing involved in navigating spaces and the people who inhabited different places in the house provided me with a sense of security that was lacking in my parents' home. On the outside, it looked like any other ordinary white two-story house on the corner of a working-class, primarily Black neighborhood of North Omaha. It had a big closed-in front porch with windows on all sides and an indoor swing on one end with a floor model TV on the opposite end that mostly showed soap operas when turned on. A cozy couch long enough to seat three to four adults comfortably sat perpendicular to the indoor swing just far enough away so someone watching TV from the sofa would not be distracted by someone watching TV while swinging on the swing. The swing moved back and forth like a glider rocking chair. As a child, I was fascinated by the indoor swing sliding smoothly along the floor, offering passengers an effortless ride. It seated two adults comfortably or three children, but typically, only adults entered the front porch, so only adults sat on the swing. The front porch was a formal space in the house. A space children could only occupy under certain circumstances.

A less attractive, small screened-in porch was in the back of the house, with a worn wooden floor covered with chipped paint. As kids, we did not use the entryway that led onto the front porch because my grandparents used it for formal greetings of strangers who might come to the door to sell something, deliver something, or check the gas meter, for example. Most of the time, however, it was a space for the patients to socialize outside their bedrooms. Children, family, and close friends usually entered the house through the back porch. We used it so much that I thought the rear porch was the front of the house for most of my childhood. It felt strange if we ever needed to enter the home through the actual front porch, which we rarely did.

The living room had a black piano pushed up against one wall flanked by shiny brown end tables with beige lamps and a big brown floor-model TV with a rabbit ear antenna on top nestled against a perpendicular wall. Our clothes could get hooked by the rabbit ears if we brushed past it too quickly without paying attention. When we were little, there was still enough space in the living room to ride our tricycles around in a circle, but as we grew, the space got smaller and smaller. The living room was designated family space and was usually inhabited by family and friends; however, not on Sunday mornings when the patients had in-home "church" in the living room or were passing through it on their way to eat in the space that doubled as a kitchen and dining room.

As a child, I secretly felt that living in a corner house was more intriguing than the houses down the block on only one street. It did not matter that when I came to Omaha, I only played with the friends who lived down the block on 28th Street most of the time. The fact that I had the *option* of playing on Pratt Street made my grandparents' house unique to me. Having the opportunity was important, perhaps even more important than exercising it. Another cool thing about living in a corner house is that I could go down the hallway to the left toward the front porch and be on Pratt Street, or I could go through the living room and kitchen/dining room to the back porch and end up on the 28th

Street side of the house. So, depending on which way I went *inside* the house, I would end up on one or the other street when I went outside. As a child, it intrigued me that I did not have to go *outside* and turn the corner to get to either street; I just had to walk in a different direction *inside*, and voilà! Like magic, I was on another street!

The patients

I saw my grandparents caring for patients daily during my visits. This meant I got to see my grandmother in her pristine, crisp white nursing uniform, cap, white stockings, and white shoes every day except Sunday—unless it was the first Sunday of the month when she wore her uniform to the church, being a deaconess and nurse on duty. Her uniform, contrasted against her flawlessly smooth dark complexion, was a visual signal that she was at work and not to be bothered with personal family stuff. That and the fact that, most of the time, we only heard her being called "Mrs. Williams" around the house by the patients indicated "do not disturb" grandma. It also meant there was a structure to our movements, eating habits, and interactions in the home. There were things I could count on, like fish on Fridays, liver on Saturdays, and chicken on Sundays. Grandpa cooked all the meals for the patients and the family. During the week, we would eat whatever was on the dinner menu for the patients, but I always knew what we were having on Friday, Saturday, and Sunday. In addition to routines, a structure meant physical boundaries.

There were places in the house that we kids could and could not use. Whenever it was time for the patients to come out of their rooms to go into the kitchen/dining room to eat, we had to go upstairs until they were seated at the table; then, we could come back into the living room that they had to pass through to get to the kitchen/dining room. The living room had three doors: one that led down the long hallway to the patients' bedrooms, one that led into the kitchen/dining room, and one that led upstairs, where the family slept except for Uncle Nels, who slept in the basement. The front porch faced Pratt Street, and because the mailbox slot was on that side, Grandma would sometimes ask a grandchild to walk down that long, narrow hall past the patients' bedrooms to get the mail off the porch when it was dropped through the slot. We could see the front porch looking down the hallway from the living room, so it felt like walking through a dimly lit tunnel with a light at the end of it if the patients had their bedroom doors, which lined each side of the corridor, closed on our trek to get the mail.

I liked the structure in my grandparents' house because it helped maintain good boundaries between the kids and the adults and the patients and the family. It was predictable, which gave me a sense of safety and emotional security. We knew what time the patients would eat, what they would eat, and where. This deter-mined when we could eat, where, and what we would eat. We never ate before the patients, always afterward. We knew that the patients' bedrooms were off limits, except for specific circum-stances, and so were their bathroom and the front porch.

The front porch was a space outside of their bedrooms where they could socialize and have visitors. But sometimes, if my aunt Doris visited, we could sit on the front porch with her and the patients and watch soap operas for a little while. That was the only time we could hang out on the front porch. Monie "Ramona," my youngest sister, fondly remembers one summer "sitting on the front porch with Aunt Doris, Grandma, and one or two patients watching *General Hospital*, wondering if Luke and Laura would ever marry."

However, going to get the mail was not considered hanging out on the front porch; we were always expected to acknowledge patients sitting on the porch when we retrieved the mail. But there was no lingering there when we retrieved the mail. We also knew the patients would never come upstairs because that was exclusively family space. The only areas in the house we shared at different times were the living room and kitchen/dining room. And that sharing was usually only brief.

On some Sundays, a preacher would come to the house and have service for the patients. That was the only time I ever saw someone play the piano in the living room and the only time I saw patients sitting there for an extended period. We had to go upstairs during their church services. We had to go upstairs when it was time for the patients to eat. We would slightly open the shiny, heavy brown door leading upstairs, peek out, and watch them walk through the living room to eat in the kitchen/dining room. We recognized most of them because they had lived in the house all our lives, but occasionally we would see a new person.

Sometimes, Grandma would close the living room door leading down the long hallway to the patients' rooms. If the door was closed, it meant a patient died, and an ambulance would pull up to the front to take the body out through the front door. If the patient did not have any living relatives or friends, that also meant that we would have to go to their funeral service at

Thomas Funeral Home on North 24th Street when the preparations were completed. I think I was about seven or eight years old when Grandma took us to the patients' funerals, and there was not any use in trying to complain about it because she would say, "That's what the Lord would want from you," and that was the end of it. Over time, I got used to sitting quietly in funeral parlors, seeing dead people in caskets, and listening to long-winded preachers eulogizing. I cannot say that I ever got comfortable with it, though. It was just something we had to do. Something the Lord expected of us to show our respects to the dead.

Patients like family

Three patients were like family to me. They were Ms. Ester, Ms. Jamie French, and Ms. Ruby Snell. Whenever the door to the hallway was closed, I hoped it did not involve them. Ms. Ester had a small, cozy, private room next to the bathroom on the left side of the hallway, and she lived with Grandma and Grandpa the longest of all the patients. When Jendayi was a toddler, Ms. Ester helped potty train her, and sometimes she would let us visit her in her room, tell us stories about her life, and show us stuff in the big black metal trunk at the foot of her bed. She was otherwise pretty private about her life. Not in a mysterious way, just a matter of fact, stay out of my business unless I invite you in kind of way. She was a nurse, too, and helped Grandma take care of the other patients sometimes. However, Ms. Ester did not wear a white uniform like Grandma but always wore clothes like she was at work when she helped Grandma. After retiring to her room in the evenings, she would change into a floral print duster and her fluffy house shoes or something similar that signaled that she was no longer at work. I guess that is how the patients knew not to expect her to attend to them after hours.

Like Ms. Ester, Ms. French also assisted Grandma with the other patients. Ms. French had a quiet, easygoing disposition with a resting smile on her face. She lived with and helped Grandma for 25 years. Sometimes when she was not working, she would watch TV with us in the family room. She was the only patient who did this, which indicated in my child's mind that she was more of an assistant than a patient. There were also times when she would leave the house to spend most of the day with her family. She was the only patient that I remember leaving the house regularly. Other patients had visitors who came over, and they would leave to go to an appointment, but Ms. French would leave to visit people. I found out, as an adult, that her son Chester would pick her up. He was her oldest son and, unbeknownst to me as a child, lived right down the street from my grandparents. He referred to Grandma as "Sister Williams" and described her as "a kind, Christian, church-going woman, and a hard worker, always working, and she knew the Lord."

Ms. Ruby Snell, a small-framed, white-haired lady with translucent skin, slept in the big front bedroom on the right side of the hallway opposite the bathroom. That room had three beds, three dressers, two rocking chairs, and a few small tables. Ms. Ruby helped Grandma wash and fold the towels and sheets. I remember her pressing the towels and sheets repeatedly with her hands, with each fold like an iron. She hardly talked at all, but she was nice just the same. I do not know how she got stuck in the same room with Ms. Pots because Ms. Pots, who looked six feet tall to me, was a mean old lady. She walked using a cane, and, if she felt especially cranky, sometimes she would swing that cane at us when we had to get the mail off the porch. Her mood seemed to vacillate between cranky and especially cranky. If she came at you using her cane like a weapon, she was especially cranky, and if she just ordered you around using her cane like a pointer, she was just cranky. Either way, I feared her, but I did not let on that I was afraid because I knew that, if Grandma needed me to get the mail, I would have to get it, whether Ms. Pots was in a mood or not.

I had to encounter Ms. Pots when I went into the bedroom to get the laundry that Ms. Ruby had folded. I would try to avoid making eye contact with her and look at Ms. Ruby to thank her, as Grandma insisted that we do while gathering the towels and sheets before leaving their room. It did not matter whether I made eye contact with Ms. Pots or not if she was in the room sitting in her rocking chair and wanted something. "Go get my Bible off that table, Gal," she would command me. "Bring me my pocketbook," she snapped, pointing her cane to direct me where to go. She barked orders like a drill sergeant. It made me wonder if she was ever in the military as a young woman. If she were especially cranky when I got the towels from Ms. Ruby, she would swing her cane at me on my way out of the bedroom. I never got hit because she always missed, but her actions told me she did not want to be bothered by a child entering her space, no matter the reason. Sometimes, Ms. Pots would ask me to go into her table drawer or inside her dresser drawers to get something for her. I had a lot of conflicting feelings about these kinds of demands because they felt invasive to me as a child, even with her permission.

Grandma taught us to respect the patients' privacy and never go into their rooms or their stuff unless she directed it or the patients permitted us to. Grandma also instilled in us respect for our elders, and Ms. Pots was older than dirt in my childhood eyes, so that was not my conflict either. I did not like being ordered around by her, and it felt creepy to go into her dresser or table drawers. Once, she called me to "get my Vaseline jar out of my table drawer over there, Gal," pointing with her cane. Later in the day, when I passed her bedroom on the way to get the mail off the porch, I saw her rubbing Vaseline all over her body like lotion, and I felt like I had just seen a *naked* person! I felt mortified! I felt like I had done something wrong. I tried to turn my head as fast as possible toward the hallway, but it was too late. I saw her, and she saw me see her. I thought I was in trouble now. When I walked back through the hallway with the mail, I made sure I looked straight ahead, and when I got to Ms. Pots' bedroom, I turned my head in the *opposite* direction toward the bathroom door across the hall and walked faster to get past her room as quickly as I could.

When Ms. Pots asked me to do personal stuff for her, it felt like a violation of the boundaries in the relationships established by my grandparents and a violation of the circumstances under which I could legitimately enter a patient's bedroom as a child. I did not like it, but I did not have the words to say how I felt nor the insight to understand my feelings. All I knew was that something was *off*, and somehow, I was implicated in that off-ness. I internalized those feelings like *I* had done something wrong. I did not know how to tell Grandma what was wrong either, so I just tried to avoid being around when it was time to get the neatly folded, hand-pressed, fresh-smelling laundry from Ms. Ruby. But that meant I would not get to briefly visit with her unless she happened to be on the front porch watching TV, which she did only sporadically. And because I was a child, I could only sit for a while and visit with Ms. Ruby if my aunt was also with me.

When we did visit briefly, conversations mainly consisted of her asking me, "How do you like school?" and asking me, "How are your brother and sister doing?" I *hated* school, but I was not going to tell her that. I wanted to ask her a million and one questions about her life, but I knew I could not do that either because another lesson from the adults was that children stay in a child's place, which means not getting up in grown folks' business. I could ask her how she was feeling and how her day was going, and that was about it. I liked being close to Ms. Ruby because she smelled like fresh, clean laundry, and sometimes, she would take my hand, place it between her hands, and pat it while talking to me. Her hands were warm and soft like cotton. She spoke slowly and gently, inviting you to sit for a while like you did not have a care in the world. I liked Ms. Ruby. I was not in town when she, Ms. French, and Ms. Ester died, so I did not get to go to their funerals, but I still treasure the memories of their presence in my life.

Death and grieving

It would be decades before I would become aware of how those early rituals of death and dying shaped my thinking about death and my approach to dealing with it. Going to a patient's funeral was almost routine because I knew what was expected of me. My grandparents did not typically talk much about patients or their lives after the funeral and burial, at least not to us kids. I do not mean this in a cruel way; I think that as a child, I never heard them. I do not recall them talking much about the living patients either, except when they spoke of the practical ways they interacted with or served them as residents in the household. It would be 26 years before someone close to me died, and nothing up to that point in my life prepared me for that.

Grandpa died when I was 34 years old. It felt like he was in the hospital one day and dead the next. I was devastated and wanted to talk about him, and Grandma was too, but it seemed like the family just took care of business like he was one of the patients. His wake, funeral, and burial were planned and implemented, and life went on without anyone saying much about him. I guess we all grieved privately in our own ways. At least, that is how I experienced it, and that is what I told myself to cope with the loneliness I felt. Nine months later, his brother, my great-uncle Nels, died. We were told he had cancer. I think he died of a broken heart, too, because my grandma had not let him visit Grandpa in the hospital or attend Grandpa's funeral. "It will be too much for Nels to handle emotionally," she claimed. I disagreed, but what would I say when my Mom, Aunts, and Uncle would not say anything about Grandma's decision? I was mad at her and them for a very long time.

I once visited Uncle Nels in the hospital, just like I did Grandpa before his death. It was hard to sit with Uncle Nels, hearing him moaning and groaning in pain, knowing I could not do anything to help him. He was hurting, and I was drowning in hopelessness. I felt paralyzed, useless, and helpless just sitting there witnessing his pain. I told him, "I'm sorry you are in pain, Uncle Nels, and I'm sorry you did not get to see Grandpa again." He continued to moan. I was reminded of being a child full of feelings and adults just ordering me around a situation without expressing much in the way of feelings about it. I did not have the words to express how I felt about witnessing death as a child, and while I counted on my grandparents and the other adults in my life to tell me what to do, I wish they had also talked about how they were feeling. It would have helped me process my feelings internally, even if the chances of saying anything about them were slim to none, growing up in a household where children were supposed to be seen and not heard.

Family

I did not get to go to my uncle Nels' funeral either, but he loomed large during my childhood. He was a tall, skinny, gentle giant to me. One of his legs and feet were twisted outward and shortened in a way that required him to sway from side to side like a rocking chair rocks back and forth when he walked. He looked like a tree blowing in the wind. He was so tall that it looked like his head touched the powerlines and streetlights overhead when I looked up at him as we walked down the chipped sidewalk. Since the Pratt Street house was also a nursing home, Uncle Nels would take care of us sometimes when Grandma and Grandpa were wrapped up in the nursing home business for many hours during the day, through the evening, and sometimes at night. We would see them regularly because we were all living in the same house, but sometimes, it was good that they were preoccupied with work because we could get away with some things without them watching us like hawks. Uncle Nels would sit on the back steps of the house in his overalls and eat an onion like

I eat an apple, bite by bite, while keeping an eye on us playing in the street. He could sit on those steps for hours without seeming bothered or bored. He would curl his long, lanky legs under him and sit. He smelled like the air in the basement when I sat next to him on the porch steps, waiting for the Tarver kids across the street to get home so I could go to their house to play. Uncle Nels' presence was a mystery in some ways. There were things I heard my grandparents say about him and many things surrounding him that they did not say, or at least not to us children anyway. The only time I ever saw Uncle Nels wearing something other than overalls was on Sundays. He would dress in nice pants and a shirt, wear his good shoes, and walk to church. He went to a different church than my grandparents. It was on the Pratt Street side of the house going east. I never knew why he did not go to Mount Moriah; I do not recall anybody talking about it. It was just treated like a normal thing.

Uncle Nels was our protector outside the Pratt Street house. He walked us to Kelly's Drugstore for candy and pop or Dairy Queen for ice cream bars on 30th Street. We were convinced there was a haunted house at the end of the street on the south corner of 28th Street and Pinkney at the opposite end of the corner of our home. We had to pass it to get to Kelly's, or we had to take the long way in the other direction going northwest to avoid it. If Uncle Nels was with us when we walked past the haunted house, we were confident that his presence would keep the ghosts and witches that swarmed around that house away from us. But, if he *wasn't* with us, we had to run past that house as fast as possible so we would not get snagged, or we would take the long route to avoid it altogether. We had to ensure we were not caught by the haunted spirits, especially when we sneaked to the store without permission. During those times, we *always* took the long route.

Nobody in the family talked about Uncle Nels' physical limitations. His impaired leg and foot were obvious but treated like they were invisible. I overheard the adults talking one day, and they said that when he was living in Arkansas—where he was born—he was run over by a wheelbarrow when he was a boy, and that is how his leg and foot got to be like that. That explanation never made sense to me, but that is what I grew up believing anyway, and because he was our elder, we certainly could not ask him directly what happened to his leg. That was grown folks' business. The other thing that was a taboo subject was Uncle Nel's intellectual capacity. He was cognitively delayed, but nobody ever said a word about that either. As a child, I realized something was off with him, but I figured that wheelbarrow must have had something to do with that, too.

When she was a toddler, he taught Monie to walk with a plastic set of toy keys. He would hold on to one key, and she would hold on to another key on the ring, and he would walk her all around the living room, and as long as he was holding a key on the ring, she would walk, but if he let go of the key, she would drop to the floor. One day, he let go of the key, and she kept walking, holding the keys in her tiny fingers as she explored the house beyond the living room. When he talked, he used words like "yonder," "git-on," and "fetch," which sounded a little bit like "country talk," but we knew what he meant. We had to be inside before the street-lights came on, and if we pushed it, Grandma would send Uncle Nels to get us. We could be over the Tarvers' house playing, and he would come up to the fence and yell to us, "Your Grandma sent me to fetch y'all," or "Y'all need to git-on in the house," or he would tell Grandma that we were over "yonder" at the Tarvers' house if he had been sitting on the steps watching us. The street-light rule was a boundary that we could nudge a little bit but not cross because it was one of the ways that my grandparents kept us safe as children. As an adult learning about sundown towns, I wondered if that history influenced the streetlight rule. Sundown towns were communities where White people prohib-ited Black people from entering after sunset.

Uncle Nels slept in the basement. As a result, it was another space in the house that we had limited access to under specific circum-stances. The basement was surrounded by concrete walls, a low ceiling of exposed wooden rafters full of spiderwebs, and a tiny, thick-paned egress window. It was damp and dark down there, even with the light on, and it always smelled like iron or some-thing you would expect to smell outside, not in a house. Uncle Nels had a bed and a dresser in the back corner, and there was a porcelain sink and an old-fashioned washing machine with a manual crank clothes wringer on top of it opposite Uncle Nels' "bedroom." An ironing board and an indoor clothesline rounded out the décor in the basement for the most part. On the front side of the basement, as you walked down the creaky wooden stairs, sat a big white wooden table that doubled as Grandpa's workbench and a place to clean fish. There were two drains on the dark grey cement floor in the basement, one near the sink and washing machine and one under the white wooden table. We never went in the basement at night if Uncle Nels decided he was ready to go to bed. We could go down there during the day to retrieve anything our grandparents wanted us to get or to hang up the wet clothes after wringing them out through the washing machine.

Grandpa's work and play

Grandpa was a quiet, gentle man, just like Uncle Nels. He rarely went on the front porch, in the patients' rooms, or in the living room unless he had something to fix in those spaces. His favorite place was outside, although he spent much time either in the kitchen/dining room, on the back porch, in the basement, or upstairs when he was ready for bed at night. We sometimes used to sit on the back porch with Grandpa and shell peanuts and shuck corn and talk about the dog and horse races he bet on when he was a betting man. Occasionally, as a child, I saw Grandpa with these booklets that looked like a magazine full of numbers in black and white print on pages as thin as a newspaper. I eventually learned that he used these booklets to bet on the horse and dog races. He would study those numbers with the intensity needed to take a test, writing in the margins of the booklet with a tiny little yellow pencil without an eraser on it. I did not know how he made the bets or find out if he won or lost. I never saw money exchange hands, and while I knew where the horse and dog tracks were because we drove past them on our way to and from different places, he never stopped at the tracks, at least not when we children were in the car.

Grandpa spent more time outside on the perimeter of the Pratt Street house. A fenced-in driveway made of loose gravel was right next to the back porch. It was big enough for one car, two dog houses, and a makeshift wire clothesline. Grandpa also stored some of his outdoor tools in the driveway, like the lawn mower. He had two brown and white hunting dogs, Princess and Sam, who lived outside in the driveway. I did not think of them as pets, and we did not play with them. They were for hunting and were a permanent part of the landscape outside the Pratt Street house. If we had to go into the driveway for any reason, it meant navigating dog poop that was typically covered with loose rocks until it eventually disintegrated into the earth. It meant ensuring the dogs did not get out when you entered or left the driveway. This task made me nervous as a little girl as I feared what would happen to the dogs if they got out and what would happen to me as a consequence. Thankfully, they never left the driveway when we were going in and out of it. Sometimes, despite having a clothesline in the basement, Grandma would hang clothes on the line in the driveway and ask us to get them once they dried. Devoted and committed to both, Grandpa spent much time in his garden at the Green House and out on Carter Lake fishing. My favorite experience, by far, was going into the basement and learning how to clean fish when Grandpa took us fishing with him. He was a patient and attentive teacher.

We caught carp, catfish, bullheads, bass, and crappies mostly at Carter Lake. Grandpa taught us how to, clean out the fish insides, make sure we removed any sacs of eggs, and cut off the head and fins of the crappies before scaling and gutting them. We pulled out all the innards and washed them inside and out as Grandpa beamed with pride about how we executed the skills he taught us. Next, we skinned the bullheads, catfish, and carp. The bass could be cooked with their heads on, but we popped out their eyes before gutting and cleaning them. He showed us how to make the bait needed to catch bass by cooking cream-styled corn and cornmeal into a slightly thick batter with a consistency that could be rolled into nice round balls that a fishhook could penetrate without breaking up the mixture. On the way to the lake, sometimes we would stop by the bait shop and pick up minnows to add to our collection of cornmeal dough and night crawlers, and we would be ready to fish. We would fish from the dock or the bank of the lake.

Grandpa was a church deacon at Mount Moriah. He sometimes had to visit sick congregants and help the pastor by leading prayer meetings or passing the basket from aisle to aisle when they collected money at church. Grandpa was deeply spiritual but was not as demonstrative about it as Grandma. He would sit and read his Bible and talk to us about God and the Bible without it sounding like a lecture or a lesson. He just spoke like he was conversing, discussing everyday life, or telling us a story. I liked learning about the Bible that way. It was much better than the insufferable vacation Bible school I had to endure frequently in the summer. Like Uncle Nels, Grandpa could typically be found sporting his overalls unless it was Sunday, and then he too would dress in slacks, a button-down shirt with a tie sometimes, and a hat, with his slick-looking dress shoes.

Grandpa was not big on watching TV, but he enjoyed baseball, and I loved watching him and Grandma banter with each other about their favorite teams. They were so relaxed and jovial with each other, teasing back and forth and joking about different players. I found the sport pretty dull, especially on TV, but I watched it with them sometimes to see them interact with each other outside of work and church. The additional time I saw them relax and enjoy each other's company was at the dinner table. Grandpa did most of the cooking and would make Grandma's food in a way that did not trigger her allergies and matched her taste preferences. He was very attentive to her needs. He planted nonacid tomatoes in his garden for her, and if he made mashed potatoes for us, he would make rice for her because she could not eat potatoes. How he kept it all straight in his head was a mystery to me because there were many foods that she could not or would not eat. I never heard him complain about it or show any sign of impatience. He just catered to her every need. I guess that is what made their 50-year marriage work for them.

He was also patient with the grandchildren. I enjoyed sitting on the porch with Grandpa, listening to him talk about his life in Arkansas and how he fished, and hunted rabbits, possums, birds, wild turkeys, and other game. He taught us how to preserve meat and store it in the ground if you don't have a refrigerator. He took us to the farm in Council Bluffs and showed us how to shoot rifles and pistols. Grandpa used to keep a rifle standing up behind his easy chair and the bullets to it in a small table drawer to the right of the chair. It was always visible. Not one grandchild ever touched the rifle or the ammunition throughout my child-hood. He taught us to respect guns as weapons for a specific purpose. Uncle Nels and Grandpa were my best male role models as a child, and I love and miss them both dearly.

Planned urban renewal/removal

The Pratt Street house was special to me. It symbolized my grandparents' hard work, resilience, and determination to succeed. One summer, when I visited them as a teenager, all the houses on the east side of 28th Street and the south side of Pratt Street were torn down. A whole neighborhood segment had been demolished in the name of "planned urban renewal." It felt like my refuge had been gutted, its innards ripped out, and its head cut off like the fish we cleaned. My vibrant childhood community became a lonely, dead-end road. The houses, trees, stores, parks, and families that were the heartbeat of the neighborhood were demolished. This planned urban *removal* project severed lifelong connections between the families and friends I spent my childhood with. Some of the most enjoyable times of my life were spent at the Pratt Street house. They are the experiences that grounded and sustained me. That shaped my worldview and influenced how I moved through and understand the world I live in today.

Chapter 4
The Tarver family

The Tarver family was at the center of the neighborhood and community between Pratt and Pinkney. They lived at 3541 28th Street until their home was demolished to build the North Freeway. Mr. Howard William Sr. and Mae Della Tarver married in 1957 and had six children, three boys and three girls—Susie, Howard Jr, Milton, Barbara, Johnny, and Caroline, a.k.a. Baby. Mr. Tarver, a Second World War veteran from Oklahoma, settled in Omaha after the war, where he met Mrs. Tarver, a nurse who grew up in Jim Crow Emerson, Arkansas, and moved to Omaha in 1944.

They built a life for themselves and their children on 28th Street that embraced and shaped the lives of families far beyond the walls of their light pink, two-story, four-bedroom house with its adjoining lot. Like Grandpa, Mr. Tarver worked at the packing house in South Omaha. He also had an in-home business as a well-respected barber. Mrs. Tarver was a licensed practical nurse, primarily working nights. Susie remembered that "When Dad came home from working [at the packing house], that's when she [Mom] would go to work. So we were never left alone." Remembering the "funny white hats" nurses used to wear, Milton said Mrs. Tarver worked until their youngest sister was born, and then she stopped working as a nurse and focused her energies on her household.

Heartbeat of the neighborhood

The Tarver home was the heartbeat of the neighborhood for the children living in the area. My siblings and I have many fond childhood memories of spending time at the Tarvers' house during our summers in Omaha. We loved it! Most of the children on the block could be found hanging out at the Tarvers' at one time or another. We swung on the wooden swing straddling their outside front porch, secured by chains suspended from the porch ceiling. We regularly played "eat the peg," a game that showed off your ability to skillfully flip a butter knife and make it land, blade down in the vast white sandpit that took up a significant portion of the backyard. Climbing up the partially cut-down backyard tree to play "King of the Mountain" was another favorite game. It demonstrated strength, flexibility, speed, and agility to see who could make it up the tree the fastest and stay there without being pushed into the surrounding sandpit below. We raced each other on the lush green lawn that blanketed their adjoining lot. We picked (and sometimes stole) big red juicy apples, not too sweet or tart, from the apple tree that lined the fence further back in the yard.

Occasionally, we would sit on the bench next to the apple tree and read books aloud or talk about anything and everything that came to our minds. We sometimes sat and watched Mr. Tarver work in their garden in the early evenings while Mrs. Tarver picked vegetables and weeded the garden. With six mouths to feed, they had every vegetable that could be grown in that garden. Hanging out at the Tarver home was nothing short of pure bliss. It was easy to lose track of time and any worries we might have had once we stepped on the other side of the fence surrounding their home. It was like walking into a magical kingdom, a fun playland with never a dull moment.

When the Tarver children played outside their fence, we always had enough kids to play baseball. We used the sewer hole in the middle of the cobblestone street as the second base and the trees diagonal to the sewer hole on each side of the street as the first and third base. The home base was anything we could find to plop down in the middle of the road opposite the second base. The third base tree was almost right in front of my second Cousin Tracy's house, who lived three doors down from my grandparents on 28th Street, and the first base tree was in front of the Tarvers' house across the street from Tracy's. Tracy had a fence around her house, too. Tracy's mom, Mrs. Ruby Smith, my grandma's niece, would sometimes sit on her front porch and watch us play baseball. She kept an eye on Snowball, their mean-ass dog, to keep her from ripping our throats out if we had to go into their yard to get a loose ball now and then. We could count on her to retrieve the ball whenever Mrs. Ruby was in the yard watering her flowers or tending to her garden.

Mrs. Ruby was one of the adults who watched out for us while going about her regular day. Her husband, Mr. Sidney Smith, worked outside the home, but she worked in her home as a beautician and was almost always around. Mrs. Ruby also pierced my sisters' and my ears as children. She did it the old-fashioned way with a threaded sewing needle sterilized with rubbing alcohol after holding it over the stove, and we had to turn the thread regularly to keep the hole from closing. Eventually, the thread was replaced with a short piece of straw from a broom burned on each end. We had to push the straw back and forth through the piercing regularly until the hole healed completely, and *finally* we could wear earrings. Each stage of the month-long process also involved slathering the earlobes frequently with Vaseline to keep the hole lubricated.

Abandoning our roots

One summer, when I visited Omaha, the Tarver family was gone, and all the houses on the east side of 28th Street had been demolished! I was devasted! It would be 40 years before I ever saw any of them again. The United States Department of Transportation, Federal Highway Administration, and Nebraska Department of Roads demolished their home and 752 others, 4 churches, and 25 businesses to construct the North Freeway (I-680) between 1976 and 1977. In ten years that started before 1973, the federal, state, and city governments ripped through the heart of the Black community with highway construction to benefit White commuters. To me, it felt like it was overnight. It felt like a part of my childhood had been annihilated.

Meeting with Susie, Milton, and Barbara was a wonderful reunion. I was eager to catch up and hear what happened after their family was forced to move out of the neighborhood they called home for many years. We sat on the lower deck of Milton's home and reminisced. From birth, the Tarver children lived in their house at 3541 28th Street, and Milton felt that "we were abandoning our roots when we had to leave our home." In Barbara's memory, "We also abandoned our dog Shaft.""Where we moved to wasn't a community. People stayed to themselves, and we stayed to ourselves because we didn't know anyone. I mean, it was just different," Susie added. Barbara fondly remembered, "When we lived on 28th Street, it was like you knew everyone. So you had a sense of belonging. And you pretty much got along with everyone. So that was a good thing." "We felt safe and supported at 28th Street."

One summer when we visited Omaha, Barbara taught Jendayi and me how to cornrow hair as it became a popular style in the United States more than ten years after actress Cicely Tyson first sported cornrows in the CBS series *East Side, West Side* in 1962. I will never forget that summer because Ms. Tyson was the first beautiful, elegant, dark-skinned Black actress I saw on the big screen. Her iconic role in the 1974 movie *The Autobiography of Miss Jane Pittman* saturated my soul and planted the seeds, unbeknownst to me then, for the genealogical research I would do in my own family many years later. Jendayi remembered how learning to cornrow helped her earn good money braiding hair in her dorm on Stanford's campus when she started college as a political science and African studies major many years later.

Milton remembered,

> Clarence across the Street, Junebug's brother, was the basketball coach. He was going to college and was like a big brother looking after all the youth, the boys, that would be per se, not the girls, but the boys. We would go to different places and play basketball. Go to the Claire Methodist Church and get us into a basketball league. The church sponsored us and gave us uniforms and things like that.

I thought about how there were always enough kids to play basketball when the Tarver kids played outside their fence, although the boys dominated the Black dirt makeshift court from the empty lot sandwiched between two houses on the other side of the block. The girls could watch the boys play basketball, or we might be able to shoot a few baskets *after* their game before one of the boys decided to take his ball. The girls played hopscotch, Double Dutch jump rope, and hand-clap singing rhymes, like "Mrs. Mary Mack, Mack, Mack. All dressed in Black, Black Black. With silver buttons, buttons, buttons. All down her back, back, back."

Milton continued, "As far as belonging, everyone knew what everyone was doing and looking out after one another, never had to worry." Pausing momentarily, he stated matter-of-factly, "You know we were poor. But you didn't feel it." Agreeing, Barbara added, "You didn't know it." "You didn't know no difference," Milton said. "But when they moved us to that other location," he frowned, "you knew the difference." Susie agreed, "You really did." Sitting up in his chair now, Milton recalled, "Now they're shunning you because, oh, you don't have a car. You take the bus …" Barbara interrupted him, "See, I never felt any of that." Unfazed, Milton continued, "Their parents were driving them where they need to go in a car, but you gotta catch a ride on a bus to get to where you gotta go, so it was like that. You knew that you didn't feel that you belonged." "The belonging was gone!" he said, reclining further back in his chair.

Barbara explained, "I didn't feel that. I guess I didn't notice it when I moved to the new place, but what made it feel like belonging, back to your original question? You had friends you could go outside and play with at our old home until the streetlights came on at 7:00." Laughing, we all remembered that family rule. "And you know," she said contentedly, "I just loved it! I loved growing up there!" She recalled, "We had an apple tree; we had a lot of things that made it feel like home." Susie said, "I loved all the kids that would come over." "We would bury each other in the sand, just play." She reminisced, "Those are the memories you never forget, how my dad would bring the sand in. And he had that sense of community and intended it to be that way."

Contrast in neighborhoods

"We moved to a working-class White neighborhood that was moving toward middle-class," Milton explained. "As we, meaning Blacks, started moving in, they, meaning Whites, started moving out of the neighborhood." In the old neighborhood, he recalled, "We were able to walk to our schools, but when we moved, at that time, the bussing started too." "So, to go to basketball practice, I couldn't walk because it was a long way away, so I had to catch this bus, and I thought, I'm going to have to quit because I'm not going to be catching this bus in this sub-zero cold weather."

Contrasting the neighborhoods, he clarified, "But on 28th Street, you can walk to Horace Mann [junior high school], you can walk to Druid Hill [elementary school], you can walk to North High. It wasn't a problem getting there, making it on time, and not being super cold, even though you are walking." Lamenting, he continued, "But now, when we moved over there on Reddick Street, it's a bus, and a transfer, and a walk to the bus stop to get to school, and …." As if things were not bad enough, Susie added, "And we had hills! It certainly changed. Yeah, it was different." Milton continued, "But yet you have a player on the same block, and their parents wouldn't offer you a ride [in the Reddick neighborhood]." "Okay, well, I gotta do what I gotta do; I gotta decide whether I continue to play or I'm going to have to stop," he remembered with resolve. "Stop came into play."

Milton had to transfer to Northwest High School after their house was taken, and it made a difference in him being successful as a student, now in a hostile, racist environment.

I asked how the schools in the Reddick area were compared to the old neighborhood, and Milton quickly responded definitively, "They did not want you there." Somewhat hesitantly, he confided, "I ended up dropping out. I didn't finish high school." Reflecting on the predominately White school environment, he shared,

> I ended up being the only Black child in the classroom. I'm sitting right up front, and every Friday, the teacher would walk right by me and hand out the test and wouldn't give it to me, and I would have to ask for it. I finally went to the counselor, saying, this is a problem; why do I have to keep asking for the test? It just kept happening. That was part of the reason I dropped out.

He continued, "They didn't want us there. The students would say it; the teachers would show it." The racial disparities Milton faced in his new school environment were not uncommon for Black students. They continued in his work environment, but he worked his way up from the bottom to achieve a successful 37-year career at Lozier, a manufacturing company, where he retired as a senior production supervisor.

Susie was older, already out of high school, and had started college when the family moved to Reddick Street. She remembered

> having to go to college and take the bus, and walking up and down the hills, and it just wasn't any fun, and I had to take more than one bus and transfer. I was at the University of Nebraska-Omaha [UNO]. They took the house right amid my transition from high school to college, which was hard for me. It was a hard transition, but then going to college was totally different than Milton's experience; still, it wasn't my old neighborhood. It would have been easier to catch the bus from my old neighborhood than from where we lived. I was learning to drive, and that was different too. I had to learn to stop on the hills and avoid sliding; it was just different! Everything was different!

Susie was thankful she could stay connected with the spiritual community outside her old neighborhood in the Benson area. Laughing happily, she shared,

> I'm still connected with the church I used to attend before we moved, but they picked me up and brought me to the church. So, it wasn't like I had to drive, catch the bus, or do anything. It was a primarily White church, and I was accepted. I had been attending that church since I was a youth, so it was a stabilizing force for me. Even now, it's still stabilizing because I was just at a ladies' retreat, and I got to see the old pastor's wife and one of their kids, who is now probably in her 40s; I don't know how old she is now. I got to see some of the folks that I knew. So that still continues and was a stabilizing force for me.

Milton said nothing stayed the same for him. It was all different. "It was a readjustment for sure," he commented. "Some of the families that started moving into the neighborhood had boys my age, so that made it a little easier," he recalled, "but it was never the same." He felt that he had to

> question their honesty, riding in someone's car you hardly know not knowing really where you are going, hearing things I don't want to hear, but yet, I go anyway, because I'm trying to find a sense of belonging because I'm on the block now. Do I want to stay at home, or do I want to venture out? I wanted to venture out.

The move to the Reddick neighborhood was not a traumatic experience for Barbara. "Like I was saying earlier," she explained,

> I don't think it was like a major trauma or adjustment for me, other than losing Shaft. I just felt like, well, this is our new house, and I didn't have to change schools. It didn't affect me. I just felt like this was business as usual. I did not like the fact that somebody's going to tell you, hey, you gotta go. I didn't like that at all! But after it was all said and done, it was something that we had to do, so I accepted it.

Susie added,

> The one thing I can say about the new home is we didn't have the big garden as we had; we didn't have the extra lot, so we couldn't form that sense of community, even if there were individuals our age, or whatever, to congregate, I didn't feel like I had any friends in the neighborhood. Right now, I don't remember anyone from that neighborhood except the next-door neighbor.

Milton remembered that there were not a lot of kids in the new neighborhood. It was mostly older adults, "and they all stayed to themselves," Susie recalled. "I don't remember anyone befriending us, taking us under their wings, supporting us, or being there for us. I don't remember any of that. I just remember I felt like I was on my own. It was time to branch off and do my own thing," she shared, her voice trailing off, quivering on the verge of tears, with compassion for herself and the family's predicament.

"Daddy didn't like the location because it was a hilly area," Milton explained. "Plus, he couldn't have the garden that he had," Susie added. "He tried, and the ground was awful, and that was important to him. And I don't remember him ever cutting hair anymore. He stopped all of that. His barber chair was stored in the garage." However, if a friend needed a haircut, once in a blue moon, Mr. Tarver would pull out his clippers. Milton remembered that, in the old neighborhood, his father's barbershop in the basement of the home facilitated his getting to know the children in the neighborhood and beyond. "He cut the hair of all the kids in the neighborhood on the weekends, and that's how I knew a lot of the folks that stayed four or five blocks away because their parents would bring the kid over to get their hair cut." Barbara recalled that *The Omaha Star* newspaper (Scoop, 2004) did a feature story about Mr. Tarver and said, "he made as much money cutting hair as he did working at Cudahy [Packinghouse]." The reporter also noted, "Howard was the only barber that I knew who could take a mirror and a pair of scissors and cut his own hair and do a real good job." Susie recalled how she enjoyed watching her father cut hair.

Family values

The Tarver family lived in the Reddick neighborhood for about 37 years until 2018. Milton shared, "Mom stayed there until we moved her into assisted living." "And then we sold the property," Susie continued. Susie moved out of the state but remembered that she would return to the old 28th Street neighborhood when she visited Omaha. "I would go back for nostalgic purposes. It was just sad. Part of my history was gone." Confirming her feelings, Milton admitted, "I do it all the time." Sheepishly, Susie confided,

> I still do it because I'm thinking, where is everybody? We don't see what we used to see. It's different. I feel like I carried that community as I moved places and had my children. Like when I lived in Milwaukee, I created our home as a safe place where their friends would come, and I would have to call their moms because they didn't want to leave.

She chuckled. "So that instilled in me what community was like. I wouldn't have had that same feeling and value if I had lived on Reddick all that time. It was definitely a value and a huge value that was lost. And the sandpile, that was my favorite place."

The family values and sayings their parents instilled in them are so meaningful the children had some of them etched into the back of their parents' gravestones at Mount Hope cemetery:

- When you point a finger at someone, there are three more pointing back at you;
- If you don't like my apples, don't shake my tree;
- If you don't have anything good to say, don't say nothing at all;

- You can send your boy to college, but you can't make him think;
- If your head weren't attached to your shoulders, you'd walk off and leave it; and
- I'm kicking, but not high.

The inscription on the front is a testament to their deep love for their parents. It reads *A Light From Our Household Is Gone. A Voice We Love Is Stilled. And A Place Is Vacant In Our Hearts That Can Never Be Filled.* Mr. and Mrs. Tarvers' light brightened the whole neighborhood.

Milton speculated that the atmosphere created by their dad was part of a strategy he employed to keep an eye on his children. He explained, "If all the other kids came over to play, that's fine and dandy, but he [Mr. Tarver] knew where his kids were." Susie remembered, "Yeah, because we had the extra lot where we played ball; that was fun. We had the garden where we grew stuff and had to learn how to till the land and the apple tree, and the thing that I miss is …" Barbara added, "And the green beans," we all laughed. Susie continued, "I mean, the thing is, I didn't eat canned goods until I went to grade school. And that's tremendous. I don't eat canned goods."

Barbara agreed,

> That's so funny. I was at the store today and was like, it's in a can, and I didn't want to buy it. Well, it's just that I know it's not good for you, and I'm like, find something in a jar; it's just going to be this one time. Just do it!

"But do you remember, Daddy, used to can, and we had Mason jars and food for the winter. So, we didn't go to the store and buy canned goods," Susie reminded Barbara. "We only went to the store to get meat, eggs, and bread, not much else," Milton agreed. We reflected on how our families' gardens of fresh vegetables sustained us throughout the year, and almost every family in the neighborhood had a garden with plenty to share with those who did not. This community tradition can be traced back to southern rural living. Susie shared that she believes her dad purposely created community in Omaha in a way similar to how he grew up in Oklahoma.

Realizing how our walk down memory lane sounded like living in paradise, I asked them if they remembered anything challenging or hard living in the old neighborhood. As they contemplated my question in thoughtful silence, Milton eventually piped up with, "It was fun! We didn't know any different. We enjoyed life and had fun. Obviously, we had disputes with some of our neighbors sometimes, but it was all said and done by the next day. So, it was no big deal. I have no bad memories." "I don't either," Susie agreed. "I'm not saying things didn't happen," she explained, "I remembered a few things happened, but they weren't anything big or major."

Pushing the idea a little more, I was curious about their experiences and memories with police, living in a predominately Black neighborhood, especially since I had no memories of police coming into our neighborhood when I visited during the summers or lived with my grandparents. Susie confirmed my memories, "They [the police] never came in our neighborhood. They left us alone." Barbara added, "Nothing was going on, so there was no reason for them to be there. I don't remember crime; I don't remember any challenges." Susie agreed, "I don't remember not feeling safe walking where we went."

Milton recalled, "The crime was there. It was on 24th Street. It was on 30th Street. But we knew where to go. Go to Dairy Queen. Go to Time Out. Go to Kelly's Drugstore and come on back home." Part of feeling safe was knowing where to go. "We had boundaries," Milton explained.

> Our grandmother lived in a single-family home on Spencer Street near the Spencer projects. So, we knew how to walk through the Spencer projects to get to her house and avoid the trouble you could run into over there quickly. We just knew how to walk through there and just keep on moving.

Eminent domain injustice

I wondered how moving to Reddick Street impacted their interactions with their relatives who lived in the old neighborhood. Milton responded solemnly, "They became phone calls." Susie offered, "It wasn't often that we could visit them. Before [the move], with my grandmother, I would see her almost every day. I would stay with her a lot. And then, walk back home and then walk to school." Milton shared,

> My aunt lived over on Ruggles Street, and I was up there almost every weekend mopping her floors to make some change. I would cut her grass. But that went away until I got older and got my car and could cut her grass again, but that broke away for a window of time because I couldn't do it because I didn't have transportation or a way to get a lawn mower over there.

Barbara reminded them that an aunt also had to move because of the highway, and she sold her house and the buyer wanted to keep the house, so moved it to a different location. They all agreed that they and some of their relatives, had a short time to move out of the neighborhood.

Remembering the injustice of the experience of eminent domain, Susie summed up that discussion with,

> Yeah, they didn't give us much time. That's what I remember. I remember it was very quick; in a hurry, you didn't have the option to say "no." Here we've lived in this house all these years, and suddenly, we have to move. I mean, it just didn't feel right. They didn't give an option. There was no choice. I remember there was some negotiation of what they would provide as funds, but I don't remember anything more than that.

She continued,

> I don't remember any help. I know Dad and Mom had trouble agreeing on where we would move and what kind of house we would get. Dad wanted to make sure there were at least three bedrooms or four. The other house had 1, 2, 3, 4 bedrooms! He wanted to make sure there was plenty enough room for everyone, and he wanted a basement also.

Milton added, "The city gave us a list of locations that met my parents' criteria. They helped out a little bit. We didn't have much time because over 100 families were looking at the same list."

As our time together wound down, we all laughed and remembered playing "Eat the peg" religiously in the sandpile in their old backyard and agreed that a foundation had been set that we all expected to experience in other places we lived. Barbara wrapped up our conversation with, "I just want to say this: if we hadn't had such fun, I would not have shown up here today." We all laughed as she ended with, "What I remember about you was your smile, your good nature, and your dimples." The Tarver family had a lasting impact on my life that set the stage for me to survive the wilderness of the White world I would be launched into every time we moved to another military base in another state as a child and throughout my adulthood, living and working in predominately White spaces.

Chapter 5
Reverend T. Michael Williams

When Mount Moriah and Risen Son Baptist Churches merged in 2019, Pastor Williams became a part of a spiritual legacy at Mount Moriah that began roughly 133 years ago. We met upstairs in the church administration office to discuss his life, ministry, and experiences in Omaha. He shared that some pastors have a friendly rivalry about whether Mount Moriah or Zion is the oldest Black church in Omaha. "Here is the deal," he explained.

> Zion has always felt like they were the older, and Mount Moriah says Zion came out of Mount Moriah, but my wife did some research in looking at the African American newspapers that were existing at the time. They tell a story that doesn't mention Mount Moriah until 1890 and mention Zion first.

Listening to him, internally, I rooted for Mount Moriah to hold the distinction of "first" as I was mentally transported back to a childhood milestone of walking down the cement steps into the underground pool below the bottom floor of Mount Moriah and being gently submerged backward, arms crossed over my chest, into the cold clear water by a pastor as he prayed for me. It was my first and only baptism. Terrified that I would drown, not knowing how to swim, it did not matter that my child body was securely supported by three adult men—the pastor and the two deacons who assisted him, one of whom covered my eyes, nose, and mouth with his big adult hand as he told me to hold my breath so I would not take in any water.

Pastor Williams continued, "When the papers mention Mount Moriah, it was around Easter, and it was the split. That split is what was Mount Pisgah and developed into Mount Moriah. So, it's an interesting story," he concluded. Hearing "Easter" brought another mental flash of dresses, patten leather shoes, socks with ruffled rims that scratch, hot comb pressed hair, and uncomfortable hats with elastic straps like those on a birthday hat. We girls had to wear these scratchy things to church *every* Easter. I hated it! But, as an adult, I loved being a member of Mount Moriah, a church that my grandparents were members of for 75 years, and a church with a rich civil rights, community outreach, and social justice history—a proud legacy that I can claim, honor, and respect. Mount Moriah provided me with a foundation and a sense of belonging, as my grandparents did, that held me up and gave me strength as I traversed, alienating predominately White spaces.

Originally from Albuquerque, New Mexico, Pastor Williams told me he is from a military family that moved around. Still, he spent from his junior year in high school to two years after college in New Mexico. He explained,

> I spent that time in New Mexico just trying to kind of figure out who I was and what I wanted to do. Then, the Lord called me to ministry. I was living in Santa Fe,

New Mexico, and the Lord just put it on my heart to come to Omaha to Grace Bible College in 1986.

As I wondered why Omaha, he shared,

I was looking at a bunch of different Bible college catalogs, and that one hit me. It was called Grace College of the Bible in 1986. It was located up on 10th Street. When I came here in August of '86, I lived at what was called The White House across from Grace College at 10th and Williams Street. That's South Omaha, "Little Italy."

Ministry and South Omaha culture

Pastor Williams completed four years at Grace, and in his junior year he started pastoring a church in South Omaha on 39th and R called Southside Baptist Church, where he encountered what he called "South Omaha culture" during the 16 years he lived in South Omaha. The sociopolitical and religious cultures he described formed European ethnic enclaves. He noted how South Omaha was so oriented to the packing house culture.

In those days, the Catholics lived in one place, the Poles lived in another, the Slavs in another; you know, they were all kind of segregated in their own communities. My church was predominately White, so there were Croatian and Eastern European people in the congregation, and they talked about where they had grown up. They called it "Goose Hollow" in relation to their family and friends that lived in that area.

According to Stu Pospisil of the *Omaha World-Herald* (2021, p. E2), South Omaha has a unique reputation for "colorful Omaha neighborhood names." Some of the nicknames include "Dog Hollow," "Goat Mountain," and "Goose Hollow," and were created by the large "enclaves of Poles, Czechs, Croats, Irish, Lithuanians and more [who] gave descriptive names to their neighborhoods" (Pospisil, 2021, p. E2). The Czech settlers had dogs, the Bohemian immigrants raised goats, and many Lithuanians raised geese, thus the name "Goose Hollow."

Seeing the surprise and curiosity on my face that a Black man was pastoring a mostly ethnic European congregation in South Omaha in the late 1980s, Pastor Williams explained,

> The reason that I went to the church in South Omaha is that the denomination had a church in Chicago that, due to white flight, transitioned from white to Black. It was called Southview Baptist Church and was located in the Southview neighborhood in South Chicago. Well, they thought South Omaha would do the same thing: transition from white to Black. So, they thought they were getting ahead of it by asking me to go to that church, but it didn't happen!

He laughed as he continued, "I think that's an interesting thing that they thought it would turn one way … because many White people left the Chicago church. And the packing house culture is also what kept White people in South Omaha."

The church moved to North Omaha in 2000 and by 2004 purchased a building on 49th and Ohio and changed the name to Risen Son Baptist Church. Curious that White people would come to North Omaha to attend church, I asked Pastor Williams if his predominately White congregation moved with him. Chuckling, he admitted, "Well, the congregation had changed some. It was not as …," he paused,

> but yes, I mean, some White folks came. We had one family that didn't come, but the others came. However, in the 16 years, the congregation did change. It started off with 70 per cent White, 30 per cent Black, and one Latino family. By the time we moved, it was 60 per cent Black and 30–40 per cent White.

He said the Latino family had a negative perception of North Omaha, so except for going to the church's 40th anniversary in the new location; they would not attend church anymore. Laughing awkwardly, he clarified, "They were good friends, but they had this perception about North Omaha." The family's decision to stop attending Pastor Williams' church because it was located in a predominately Black community is an illustration of how white supremacist ideology can be internalized and acted upon by anyone, regardless of racial background.

Pastor Williams continued, demonstrating the church's outreach ministry and Black capacity-building efforts within the North Omaha community:

> The church was on 49th and Ohio, and down 52nd Street was Fontanelle Elementary School. The church had a couple of folks who volunteered at the school, including myself. From that, we established an after-school program related to child evangelism fellowship [CEF]. CEF has what we call good news clubs. We did good news clubs in that school and had a relationship over a few years. I got to know families and got to know

parents and was involved, through Omaha Together One Community, in setting up a parent-teacher group in the school. We had good relationships with the principals so that we could do some things: support and develop relationships with the people, such that my wife started a dance group at church with the kids that were coming. We felt very good about it, and it was like, this is where we need to be.

Proud of the program's impact, he explained, "It's CEF for short, and if you look it up, it's the largest ministry to children in the world. There is work being done in every country except North Korea." Black churches have a long history of not only providing for the spiritual needs of Black communities but also the social and economic needs as well. A tradition that dates back to enslavement and has sustained Black families in the continued face of anti-Black racism.

Modern North Omaha

Pastor Williams met his wife when the church moved to North Omaha, and they live on 56th Street, just north of Ames Street. Familiar with the area, I shared that I used to live over there. "Okay. Yes, so it's a nice area. Pretty quiet. It's not probably traditional North Omaha, but it is more modern times North Omaha." Puzzled by the descriptors "traditional" and "modern" North Omaha, I asked him to explain.

Pastor Alvin's father pastored Zion in the 1960s and 1970s, and he tells me about North Omaha not being past 42nd Street. So, I think of North Omaha basically as

Dodge to Sorenson, 72nd to the river. He thinks about it as the river to 42nd Street. So, that's what I think about when I say "modern" North Omaha. And I've read some of the history and how it was very segregated and tight-knit, too!

Sharing his perceptions of modern North Omaha when he moved there, Pastor Williams said,

It was welcoming. I'll say that. The man on the one side we lived next door to was a pastor. He had been president of the NACCP when I first came here. Dr Reynolds, I don't know if you know that name, but anyway, across the street, a couple with a little boy, he worked for one of the banks, and I don't know what she does, and they were both doing well. There are a couple of houses where they continue to turn over, and the house on the other side of us has been one of those. Then, behind us is a woman my wife has always been friends with. The other thing is there were about five, six, seven pastors in that neighborhood.

Curious, I asked him what he attributed to so many pastors living within the same area.

I think it was because it was a safe, quiet neighborhood. It was not an upper-class neighborhood, but you know, it was a comfortable neighborhood. Let me say that, yes, that's a good word, a comfortable neighborhood. There were a couple of those families that you mentioned that your grandparents wouldn't let you play with, but there were also a lot of different church members and pretty decent families when we first moved there. What I mean by that is just people doing their best, living a good life kind of thing.

In some ways, Pastor Williams described a modern neighborhood like the mostly working-class homeowning neighborhood I grew up in, in "traditional" North Omaha. A community of hardworking Black families living, trapped by systematic white domination in a racially segregated geographical space, doing their best to support themselves and create a comfortable life for the next generation.

Their efforts are consistent with what Geter (2022) defines as "The Black Period"—a world in which Blackness represents possibility and a modicum of freedom in a world otherwise full of lies and myths about Black life. The Black Period provides a counter-narrative to the onslaught of negative stories of Black life constructed by White America. The Black Period, created by Black parents, grandparents, aunties, uncles, cousins, neighbors, friends, and pastors, offers Black children positive, productive, mental, physical, and social imagery that can open the mind, body, and spirit to see options and opportunities.

The Black Period does not shield Black children from the harshness of life circumstances or protect them from the grief and sadness associated with losses, as these are the complexities of what it means to live. It can, however, help them discern at a deep level that being in a Black body is not the problem, and it might help them minimize the internalization of the white supremacist narratives that fuel the structure of American life. The Black Period is what my grandparents created for me during the summers

I visited them and later when I lived with them to attend college. The Black Period is what our neighbors, the Tarvers, the Smiths, and other families created for each other.

Shifting demographics and safety

"It has changed," admitted Pastor Williams, sounding resigned as he let the reality sink in. In fact, he continued,

> On 52nd Street on the corner of Larimore, on the south-west corner of Larimore, there is this house; I used to watch this guy; every time I turned the corner, he's out there cutting his yard, he's an older man, and he and his wife had been there for a long time and raised their kids and all that. Well, he got to the point where he couldn't do that anymore, and he couldn't take care of the place, and the kids didn't want the place, so now four Asian families are living in that house. The Asian population has increased. Actually, the White population in our neighborhood has increased, and the Black population has decreased.

Listening to the shifting demographics, it sounded like the neighborhood was transitioning into a racially integrated space. I asked Pastor Williams if he would describe the neighborhood as initially middle class and Black but now shifting more towards working-class and more racially integrated. "Yes, that's very, very accurate. It's probably not as middle class anymore," he explained.

What happens to historically Black middle-class neighborhoods when individual choices driven by economic successes and

failures instead of city planning and policy shift the demographics of the community? I have been socialized to believe that
integration is always good for society, an indicator of racial and
economic progress, and a sign of social and cultural advancement. Are there downsides to integration? Could what Pastor
Williams described in why the neighborhood is changing be
called de-gentrification?

Gentrification is often defined as the displacement of predominantly poor and Black long-term residents in a neighborhood
by young, affluent White people. In this case, some long term
Black middle-class families, no longer able to afford their homes,
are being displaced by White and Asian working-class families,
creating a racially and economically mixed neighborhood with
fewer Black homeowners. Is this what de-gentrification looks like
when it is driven by racialized capitalism?

Black families continue to bear the brunt of the wealth gap created by the racial inequities of redlining, and economic down-
turns exacerbate their difficulties. However, some middle-class
Black families have also maintained a secure financial base and
can insulate themselves during times of recession. Nevertheless,
a once middle-class home-owning Black community is being
gradually erased and replaced by White, Asian, and Latinex
working-class renters in homes repossessed by White banks and
real estate institutions that engaged in predatory race-based
lending practices while claiming to be "colorblind" with their policies and practices.

Pastor Williams reflected on what might be contributing to the
demographic shifts.

I think some of it has to do with broken relationships. Like this house I was telling you about, the kids didn't need the place. So, they are doing well enough that they didn't need the house, so they just sold it, and that's that. But on the other hand, others aren't doing as well and can't afford to stay in their homes. The economics of the society have impacted their ability to stay there. As a matter of fact, a young Black man bought the house next to us, the one that I told you has changed. We talked while he cut the grass, and he had aspirations for that house. But he was on the edge [economically] a little bit, got himself in a bind, and had to leave the house. Couldn't keep it. And he was buying it! And the other thing I would say is on the other side, the house that Pastor Reynolds lived in, there's a third family in there now, I think, and none of them have been Black.

Thinking about the safe, quiet, middle-class neighborhood he experienced in 2004 when he moved to modern North Omaha, I asked Pastor Williams if that climate changed with the shifting demographics. After a long pause, he said softly, "Uh, just a little bit. I'm thinking more about the people walking up and down the street." "People without stable housing in the community?" I inquired in an attempt to clarify what he said. "Well," he paused again,

I don't know that I'm saying that. I'm saying not so much that people are experiencing housing instability, although if you talk to Pastor Cheeks on the corner of Ames and 56th Street, she would say a lot of unhoused people. But for me, I'm thinking more about safety. And I'm thinking about the people that are walking past the house. I think they are coming from somewhere, going somewhere for the most part. But you wonder more than you used to about them breaking in.

After another long pause, he offered, "There are probably more people using public transportation. That's a good description."

"Walking to catch the bus?" I asked.

> That's exactly right. Yeah, there's probably a little more of that, and I'm thinking even more of the young men and women that walk past; that's just a little bit different feel than it used to be. For instance, one of my frustrations is there's a gas station on the corner at 56th and Ames, and they'll get a "miniature" [small bottle of alcohol], and by the time they've gotten to my house, they're finished with it, and they'll throw it in my yard.

Getting a vivid picture of how his neighborhood was changing, I asked Pastor Williams if he noticed any other changes. He continued,

> Yes, and I'm saying, too, if you get kids going down to the gas station to get candy or whatever, they'll throw their wrappers down in front of my house, and there was a time when I'll say, "Could you please pick that up?" I don't know if I would say that today. You know. That kind of thing. It's just a little different.

I agreed that times have changed, and the days of knowing your neighbor seemed to be slipping away. "Nowadays, you say, 'Please pick that up,' and instead of a 'Yes, sir,' you are liable to get cursed out or get a gun stuck in your face," I quipped. "Exactly!" We both laughed, half joking and half serious. "Yeah! Yeah! And they never said 'Yes, sir,' but they were nice enough to pick it up and look at me. They didn't say it, but they had that look of 'I'm sorry,'" Pastor Williams clarified. These were the things that raised questions about his safety and comfort and the well-being of his wife.

Intergenerational cultural differences seem to account for some of the differences Pastor Williams described. When communities mainly were segregated with long-term residents of similar cultural backgrounds, families were more likely to share the same or similar values and approaches to rearing their children and looking out for each other, creating a cohesive community culture of safety, familiarity, and comfort. However, that cohesion can be disrupted with the infusion of new residents of different backgrounds into a neighborhood. New and possibly different family values shape how people show up in the community and interact with each other. Could this be a downside of integration? When a community becomes integrated racially, economically, or culturally, how do neighbors attempt to maintain some degree of community cohesiveness? How do our biases and prejudices shape a sense of community belonging when a neighborhood is experiencing shifting demographics?

Pastor Williams recalled sharing a story about his granddaughter,

> And I'll tell you. When she was about seven, my granddaughter and another little girl who had been coming to our church sold lemonade, and people were so supportive they just gave them the money. They ended up making about 40 dollars that day. And we were like, "What!?!" Surprised and pleased. And I'm not saying that

the same thing wouldn't happen today, but I don't know if I would feel as safe with them being out there today. And I don't know that we paid a whole lot of attention. I mean, we paid attention, a peek here and there, but we would want to be out there with them more so today.

"In some ways," I offered, "we are not just talking about your neighborhood." "Or the community," he added. "It's the society. Because the societal trends, economics, and what the jobs are doing play a big part." His critique and experiences made me think about how the changing racial and class composition in US cities led to not only White flight but also Black flight as middle-class Black people fled to other neighborhoods with signs of economic decline and perceptions of safety and comfort (Woldoff, 2011). I also thought about the role of the media in shaping perceptions of neighborhoods in North Omaha, as the story of his friends who left his church when it moved to North Omaha continued to linger in the recesses of my mind.

Media representations of North Omaha

Given the power of the media as an agent of socialization and influence, I asked Pastor Williams how he thinks media representations of certain communities and groups impact perceptions of how people are experienced in North Omaha and whether he has witnessed any shifts in media coverage of North Omaha. "That certainly plays a big part," he shared.

I think the media are people. And they have perceptions, and they do their media based on their perceptions. And so, if they have a racist bent, the media is racist. And it certainly is. And if they have a political bent, then the media bends one way or the other. I didn't get her, but I reached out to the WOWT news director about three or four weeks ago when it first came out that Trump pleaded not guilty. The six o'clock WOWT news headline said, "Trump not guilty."

Agreeing with the pastor's response to the headline, I scoffed, "Which is certainly not the same thing as he *pleaded* not guilty."

He shared another example of media bias.

We were involved in trying to keep Nebraska from having a voter ID law. Channel 7 came to our press conference on that but didn't ever say very clearly, didn't use our voices, didn't use our pictures, and had the voice-over, and didn't clearly say; these people are asking you to vote *No*. Yet, they interviewed the Secretary of State, who favored this, and it lasted a couple of minutes. And he clearly said, more than once, that people should support this. And I got that news guy. And he hemmed and hawed and said, "You see that distinction?" Yeah! I see that distinction! There are some other examples, so that's clearly a bias, especially in this community where I think there are people who want and need to have North Omaha be less than.

Racially biased, inaccurate, and stereotypical representations of Black people and communities by the media date back to the late seventeenth century with the production of minstrel shows on the American theater stage. These racially offensive depictions by White actors wearing black makeup, wigs, and body prosthetics perpetuated White supremacist stereotypes of Black people as ignorant, criminal, lazy, deviant, and subservient to White people. This "less than" depiction of Black communities continued in the film industry into the early 1900s when White Hollywood filmmakers limited Black actors to roles like maids, chauffeurs, criminals, and predators. By the late 1960s and 1970s, these negative stereotypical roles extended to include the construction of Black communities in the era of "blaxploitation" films as full of pimps, drug dealers, gangsters, prostitutes, and perpetual violence.

White political candidates reinforced these stereotypes with racist campaign rhetoric and slogans using terms like "welfare queens" and "super predators" and framing predominately urban Black neighborhoods as drug and crime-infested to justify "law and order," "war on drugs and poverty" legislation that did virtually nothing for Black communities economically and socially but fed the Prison Industrial Complex with the mass incarceration of Black men, women, and youth (Valandra and Leslie, 2022). Unfortunately, by white supremacist design, these negative stereotypes of Black life have persisted in society and extend across all forms of media, including news reporting.

"I remember in Sociology 101 something about societies always having something to look up to and something to look down on. And because of the color of our skin, that's what that is," Pastor Williams observed.

> And at least it's been in Omaha since I moved here. The interesting thing is that they [the media] will move with the trends and hire Black folks, but they are only going to go so far in telling the truth or exposing it.

Pastor Phillips, president of the New Era Baptist State Convention, Willis Brown, and I, as President of the IMA [Interdenominational Ministerial Alliance], met with the editor at the *Omaha World-Herald* [newspaper] because we felt that they were presenting too much negative news about North Omaha. They acquiesced a bit and did a couple of positive stories within the next two weeks. But still, the overall trend is people have a negative perception of North Omaha, to the point that we are working with some organizations to try to change that.

Black notes

Pastor Williams explained he is working with organizations like Civic Nebraska, church organizations, the New Era Baptist State Convention, and the NAACP in his role as its current president to address the negative perceptions of North Omaha. "We already understand that White folks don't want to come here [North Omaha]," he explained, "but the idea is to bring White people from West Omaha, Black people from North Omaha, and folks from East Omaha together in conversations around things that are critical to people in North Omaha." He elaborated on the details of implementing the plan. "We are holding the meetings at UNO because White folks are scared and don't feel comfortable in North Omaha." Laughing at the ludicrousness of it all, he remembered, "When we did the MLK [Martin Luther King] celebration for IMA, White people would come to Salem [Black Baptist church located at 31st and Lake Street in North Omaha], but they would not come here [Mount Moriah, located on 24th Street in North Omaha]."

Listening to the activist efforts of Pastor Williams and his colleagues to change White people's perceptions of North Omaha, I reflected on the irony and hypocrisy of White fear of Black spaces within the historical and contemporary context of the ongoing White brutality and violence inflicted on Black bodies since the founding of this country. For centuries, Black people have devised ways to survive the violence of the white power structure. We continue to strive in the face of police brutality, denial of education, inadequate health care, and restricted access to the capital necessary to acquire land, housing, and jobs essential to building intergenerational wealth for our families.

Black people have always had to contend with white legislative and judicial violence affecting our access to safety, equity, fundamental freedoms, resources, and life itself in America. White people are afraid to attend a Black church located on 24th Street for a few hours, but Black people are expected to live with the ever-present reality of White supremacist and anti-Black violence for generations! And we do live with it, along with any violence that may surface within the community, employing multiple methods to survive and thrive, as Pastor Williams described in his ministry and activist work in North Omaha.

In her book *Ordinary Notes*, Sharpe (2023) describes these efforts of Black care as "freedom methodologies" designed to realize joy and inspiration in a world intent on destroying Black life. According to Sharpe (2023), such methodologies are the Black notes necessary to facilitate push-back, inspiration, and imagination, cultivating living a Black life in freedom. Pastor Williams' challenge of media representations of North Omaha is also a

Black note of resistance to the erasure of Black activism and the distortion of voter ID legislation that would have negative ramifications for Black life. Black notes can save Black lives.

Living in North Omaha as a young woman, I witnessed plenty of examples of Black notes in the efforts of our neighbors to care for their families and sustain our community. Neighbors planted gardens and shared their harvests, watched each other's children walk to and from school, attended church revivals and outreach ministries, supported black-owned businesses through patronage, and subscribed to the Black-owned and operated newspaper *The Omaha Star*. Families worked two and three jobs to make ends meet and to save enough money to send their children to college, buy a new car, purchase a home, or make repairs when they were systematically denied bank loans.

They passed their values of spirituality and a strong work ethic, the importance of education, and respect for oneself and others to subsequent generations. These everyday, ordinary Black notes fostered a sense of belonging and community cohesion. They are the notes that facilitate individual Black achievement and success. The notes that Sharpe might describe as imperceptible to the white power structure are effective in fueling and affirming Black life in segregated spaces. Despite the best efforts of Black families, however, racial and economic segregation and under-development of Black urban spaces continued to be pervasive.

Chapter 6
Linda Hill

Connection

I met Linda in the women's locker room at the downtown YMCA, where I swim during my visits to Omaha. "I've never seen *you* here before!" Linda asserted, noticing me while she prepared to leave the locker room. I interpreted her emphasis on "you" in two ways. We were the only two Black women in a white space. She was telling me that she had never seen me personally and she had never seen another Black woman in the locker room before. Laughing, I responded, "That makes two of us." I had never seen another Black woman in the locker room or the pool, for that matter, since I started swimming at the YMCA about a year ago.

Curious now, she wanted to know more, so I told her I was writing a book about North Omaha. She offered, "You should interview me. I've lived here for over 62 years, and I've seen a lot." Now, I was curious. She continued, "I can tell you one thing that hasn't changed since I've been here: the prejudice." Her declaration coincided perfectly with the exit of the White women from the locker room and reminded me of what my grandmother said about Omaha when she and my grandfather first moved there in 1944.

Linda's openness and courage to discuss racial prejudice while in a public White space was refreshing and inviting for me to experience. She signaled immediately that she was not hampered by the coded language I have witnessed Black people use, including myself, when talking about race or racial issues in the presence of White people or public white spaces. In a few short minutes, she cut through formality. She tapped a familiar chord that has reverberated for centuries almost unconsciously as Black people have collectively navigated the realities of living with anti-blackness and white supremacy. Her boldness intrigued me.

From Bermuda to North Omaha

Linda was born on the island of Bermuda and moved to North Omaha on August 10, 1961, as a 13-year-old when her mother married her stepfather, who was stationed at Offutt Air Force Base. Her family lived on Franklin Street the first year they lived in Omaha. She recalled that when they moved into their house at 3377 Erskine Street, they were the first Black family to move into that area, and "the White people took off," she said, laughing. As White flight continued, Blacks were able to buy the houses left behind. Linda shared, "My mother bought our house for $11,000. The White people were moving into the Benson area and the big homes near Tech High. From Crossroads to Boys Town, it was nothing but cornfields then."

It was not hard for me to imagine that the well-developed White West Omaha area that I grew up with in the early 1970s was once nothing but cornfields. Linda went on to describe how, as White people fled, Black people were able to purchase affordable homes in the area. Her family's experience was similar to that of the Tarver family in the late 1970s. They were forced to move and ended up in a neighborhood transitioning from White to Black homeowners after the city took their original home to construct the North Freeway. Linda has four sisters and described herself as a "staunch Democrat who became a citizen the year Jesse Jackson ran for president in 1984." She recalled him coming to Omaha to speak at the library, saying, "It was pouring down that day with rain, but when he got up to speak, the sun came out very bright." She was prompted to become a citizen after his presidential campaign.

Linda described her mother as very industrious, "My mother opened a daycare in 1978 called Dots and Tots, one of the first Black-owned daycare centers in Omaha."

Her mother paid $4,000 for the house she converted into a daycare center. It had a beautiful orange sign that read, "Dots and Tots," and below the title were the words "Jesus loves the little children. All the little children of the world. Red and yellow, black and white, they are precious in His sight." She also worked three jobs and maintained the daycare until she retired at 62 years old. Her mother lived in her home on Erskine Street for 50 years until she died on May 17, 2012.

Housing and gentrification

Linda recalled that 60 years after the Omaha riots, Habitat for Humanity built many homes in North Omaha, and Holy Name Church also built many homes. After the riots in the late 1960s, many White-owned businesses left the Near North Side. Still, many low-income and working-class Black families and business owners did not have the means to move from the area. They were systematically denied access to residential and commercial loans outside of the Near North Side.

Disinvestment, deterioration, and disjointed redevelopment projects became the norm for the next couple of decades. In the early 1980s, depressed prices in the area started mainly attracting White investors, private nonprofits, and city planners. They collaborated to rehabilitate North Omaha to "attract people with a higher income back to the community, whether they be black or white," according to Alvin Goodwin, founder and president of the Omaha Economic Development Corporation (Kotoz, 1983, p. 4-A.)

Astute, Linda recognized the impact of continued "rehabilitation" efforts decades later and shared, "My mother owned our house since 1962. Now what are we experiencing?" She questioned rhetorically, throwing her hands in the air in frustration. "Look at all these buildings!" As her voice continued to rise, she noted, "Now it's the Africans and the Mexicans, the Asians, and the Whites that are living in all these beautiful homes and not us! So, that has to do with gentrification." She continued, offering her explanation of what was happening. "White people didn't want us living here in the first place, and they are not coming back to live; they are just coming back to own, and they find different little ways to take over again by selling to everybody except Black Americans."

Her observations coincide with what Richard Cottage, then supervisor of the city housing rehabilitation effort, reported experiencing in 1983. He told Kotoz (p. 4-A) that "young white couples have been contacting him to find out how to get information on buying rehabilitated homes on the Near North Side." North Omaha is experiencing another wave of gentrification framed as "redevelopment," this time with more than young white couples moving to the Near North Side.

Linda continued to share ways she believes White people and institutions undermine Black life. "My mother had the house in my stepdad's name. And follow this timeline," she directed me. "Follow me closely," she repeated to underscore the point she was about to make. "He died on April 19, 2004. The insurance wrote her a letter saying she inherited the house." Pausing to look directly at me, Linda continued.

> I made two copies of that insurance letter, and Mom took it to a lawyer to put the house in her name so that when she died, she could leave it to my younger sister Carol. But she could never put the house in my sister's name. The insurance company and the lawyer were, obviously, in cahoots.

I was silently puzzled over the dynamics that prevented her mother from making her daughter the legal heir to her property. Incredulous now, Linda shared what happened next. "My sister was sitting in the house one day, smoking her cigarettes, and the sheriff came and put her out of the house, just like that, and put a padlock on the door." Emphatically, she stated, "It's clearly my mom's house, and clearly they were married! She lived in that house for 50 years!" After that experience, her sister Carol had a mild heart attack. Linda maintained that "They killed her because a couple of years later, she died from a massive heart attack." Essentially, Linda's mother's house was stolen from her through a white power structure designed to deceive and exploit working-class and low-income Black families.

In some ways, Linda gave voice to a similar phenomenon that Pastor Williams witnessed in his neighborhood in "modern" North Omaha. Other families of color are displacing Black families, and the homes are sold by mostly White builders and private investors living outside of the community. When she retired at 62, Linda lived on a $400-per-month pension. She did not have much money and could not keep the home she owned for 33 years because she could not pay the taxes after she retired. In Nebraska, property that becomes delinquent is sold at auction to whoever pays the delinquent taxes. Linda explained, "A white man paid the $2,000 tax that was owed and bought the house out from under me."

"That day, I went downtown and talked to Douglas County Treasurer John Ewing to explain my situation. He says, 'Well, since you are 64, you could go before a judge, and they will probably work something out with you.' Well, that never happened," she explained. Because the property taxes were delinquent, Linda was expected to pay the whole $2,000. She said, "They wouldn't accept a penny less. So, I lost it, and a white man took over my house." The new house owner rented it to Linda for the next 11 years. Despite being a stable homeowner for 33 years, Linda lost the equity in her home to a White man who bought it dirt cheap with the assistance of the government. Linda and her mother were victims of an intergenerational pattern of legal property confiscation—a familiar experience faced by low-income Black land and homeowners, interrupting their ability to experience basic economic security and wealth accumulation.

To Linda, gentrification extended to public Black spaces as well. She was less than impressed with the Omaha City Council and Mayor Jean Stothert's plans for urban redevelopment of Adams Park. She said, "Under the mayor's tenure, the City stripped Adams Park, located at 3121 Bedford Avenue in North Omaha, of its basketball court, baseball diamond, football field, and swimming facilities, and the Gabrielle Union Pond that was named in honor of the Omaha native actress." The park, frequented by primarily Black families living in the area, was victim to the Omaha Chamber of Commerce urban planning scheme to promote "redevelopment" in the area. "Now, do you know what is in Adam's Park?" Linda asked sarcastically. "Concrete walking paths and grass," she said flatly. She felt it was dehumanizing and the city was treating Black people the way they were treated during slavery, as chattel.

Education and working while Black

Reflecting on her childhood, Linda stated, "I did very well growing up in North Omaha. I was very popular in school. I was a cheerleader at Tech High for four years. I was the fastest typist at Tech High then, only taking typing in 9th and 10th grade. I graduated in 1967." Linda focused on business courses while at Tech High, taking bookkeeping and shorthand and typing and using an adding machine. She said, "Black students who graduated from Tech High then did very well in the job market. I worked as a switchboard operator at Tech High in my 11th and 12th years." Linda declared enthusiastically, "It is like I was born to be a secretary!" and shared that, when she worked at the telephone company, they required workers to perform 10,000 strokes an hour. She could do 20,000 strokes an hour as a key puncher. Laughing, she said, "It was like I was born to hit keys!"

I mentioned that I found her ability to remember exact dates remarkable. Laughing again, she responded, "It must be in my genes." Linda worked at Mutual of Omaha for two years and then moved around to better-paying jobs as she heard about them. She worked for Union Pacific Railroad for nine years from 1979 to 1988 and then for Omaha Public Power District (OPPD) at the power station in Fort Calhoun as an executive secretary for Design Engineer Nuclear (DEN) from November 1988 to October 11, 2001.

When she entered her 50s, things changed for her in the workforce. Linda said that the government required companies to hire Black employees in the office beyond janitorial and outside yard work as part of Affirmative Action policies. Still, companies were trying to find ways to "get rid of Black employees." As an example of workplace prejudice, she explained, "I was a key puncher at Union Pacific Railroad and was suddenly demoted to a janitor position. Then I was told I had to work in the railroad yard as a 'forkliftologist' and then as a jitney driver." She felt the company's efforts to get rid of her continued when they tried to send her to St Louis, even though there was a requirement that you could not expect a worker to travel that far for a job. She said, "I heard there was a lot of gang violence in St Louis, and I had two boys in high school, so I did not want to go there. I told them 'no' and took the company buyout of $30,000 and started working for OPPD in August 1988."

She recalled having a boss at OPPD that she said "Was on me like white on rice." Her White boss would not let Linda go to her grandmother's funeral, telling Linda, "That was your step-grandmother." Linda told her, "I've never heard of that terminology. She has been my grandmother for 40 years." Linda was fired from OPPD because she called her boss a bad name. The company accused Linda of being prejudiced. She noted with regret, "My boss pushed me to that limit." She went to her grandmother's funeral but said she never recovered from the firing at OPPD.

Linda worked for 42 years, mostly in offices, retiring at 62. She shared that the good jobs she had afforded her, as a single mother, the opportunity to provide her boys with a faith-based education at Holy Name Elementary School in the heart of North Omaha off Fontenelle Boulevard and Creighton Preparatory High School, a private Jesuit school for boys in Omaha. She said she wanted her boys to have a faith-based education because "public schools don't teach religion like all the schools did in Bermuda when I lived there." Linda is very proud of her sons and shares the same birthday with her oldest. He is 55 years old and lives in Omaha. Her youngest son, who lives in Arizona, is a supervisor for the city of Scottsdale and runs his own heating and air conditioning business.

God and the burning house

On March 26, 2023, the home that Linda lived in at 3371 Erskine Street for 44 years burned down. It took her two months to find a new place, and she has lived at her current address, "a stone's throw away from the previous house," she said, for eight months. Her husband told her his cell phone was the cause of the fire. It was on a Sunday, and she was at church when the house caught fire. Sharing how she experienced the loss of her home, she said, "God is good, but I felt like Job from the Bible at first." She did not have any insurance, and all her church clothing burned. Her neighbors and church community stepped up to help. She explained their generosity, "My pastor told me that I'm so nice to people that turn around is fair play. Everything they gave me was new—furniture, dishes, everything."

Linda is a member of Zion Baptist Church. She described it as "A historical church, 135 years old and the third oldest Black Baptist church in the state of Nebraska. St John's African Methodist Episcopal church, next door to Myers Funeral Home, is the oldest AME in Nebraska." Linda described her relationship with the church: "I'm the type of person who never left the church." She elaborated, stating that people say, 'My mom made me go to church when I was little. Now I'm grown; I'm not going to go anymore.' That is not me. I never stopped going to church from the age of two in Bermuda."

Linda continued to profess her faith, stating, "I believe in God the Father, God the Son, and God the Holy Spirit. God never lies. If you trust Him in everything, God reigns over the bad and the good." Using her religious values to make meaning of her house burning up, Linda shared,

> Like, my house burnt, and people said that was karma.
> No, it wasn't karma; it was God's intention that it would
> happen. And even though I lived there for 44 years,
> I have my memories, but I don't miss the things because
> I am better off now. God had that in His mind all along.

She said two large dumpsters were used to discard the things that burned up in her house, and she still had to downsize to move into her new apartment.

The best land and spiritual faith

I asked Linda what she finds appealing about Omaha that she stays here despite the prejudice she has experienced and witnessed by some White people. She responded, "To me, it has the best land. We are close to the river; we are close to the airport. We are close to downtown. We are close to the highways." She testified unequivocally, "If God is for you, nobody can be against you!" Linda then talked about what she did not like about Omaha.

> I think it is just terrible that we have this Black-on-
> Black crime. We don't have to worry about the Ku Klux
> Klansmen anymore. We are killing each other. And
> I attribute that to three generations not going to church.
> The children don't listen to their parents. The parents let
> the children do the parenting. They don't have any val-
> ues. It's a breakdown of family values. They don't know
> the basic Ten Commandments—thou should not kill,
> thou should not steal, thou should respect your parents
> and love everybody!

Linda believes it would be a beautiful world if everybody could live by the Ten Commandments.

In her practice of spiritual faith, Linda said, "As Christians, we cannot just sit in the church and pray that people will come. We must go out where they are and encourage them to attend church and study the Bible." She is a part of several missions at Zion. If she could have things her way, no liquor stores would be open on Sundays, and there would be no sports. People would go to church on Sundays. "That's how it was in the old days," she chuckled. "At least God gave us six days. We could give Him one day." Linda's faith and ongoing connections with family, friends, and her church have been a source of resilience and strength, guiding her since childhood and paving the way for her to weather the storms of white supremacy. She faces setbacks with courage, faith, and determination, allowing her to create opportunities for her sons to fulfill their dreams and aspirations.

PART III
Neighborhood, inheritance, and legacy

Chapter 7
History of the North Freeway and city planning

History of the North Freeway

Along with the history of discriminatory federal, state, and local housing policies and private practices, the nation's interstate highway system has been and continues to be used by the White power structure as a tool to physically and economically isolate Black communities (Archer, 2020). Scholars of urban planning and transportation (Archer, 2020; Fotsch, 2007) contend that the construction of the interstate highway system played a key role in creating spatial and economic conditions prevalent in urban centers today—conditions that influence interracial interactions, economic mobility, and community stability. Archer (2021, p. 2127) noted that "transportation policy has always been a driver of inequality. The nation's transportation system, like other American systems, has been deployed to maximize the oppression of Black America while accelerating the accumulation of political and economic power in white communities." North Omaha is no exception.

Construction of the North Freeway began during the 1960s and was planned for completion by the mid-1980s (United States Department of Transportation Federal Highway Administration and Nebraska Department of Roads, 1975). Controversy and opposition to the North Freeway were immediate and ongoing, continuing today. Unsurprisingly, the freeway that would have connected to I-680 was stopped when wealthy White residents living in the North 30th Street neighborhoods of Florence and Miller expressed their concerns, persuading the Nebraska Department of Roads planning board to consider alternative routes that would not split their community. However, the opposition mounted by the predominantly Black community restricted to the Near North Side, and their allies were ignored by the planning board.

Some African American residents favored the North Freeway's proposed pathway, and some White residents opposed it, including some City Council members. Prominent leaders in the Near North Side Black community, like Preston Love, Jr and former Senator and City Council member Brenda Council, disapproved of the North Freeway. One of the most persistent vocal opponents of it was Senator Ernie Chambers. He represented the 11th district of North Omaha for 46 years and is the longest-serving and first African American state senator in Nebraska history. He is also a long-term resident of North Omaha, having had a barber shop business in the area for decades. Former Senator Chambers challenged the legality of the freeway and the use of state funds for federal interstate projects. The Nebraska legislature responded by changing the law so that the freeway bill could be passed without violating state funding laws.

Former Senator Council argued that the resulting displacement of African American families from the area would be a "brain drain" on the community, reversing efforts made to improve high school and college graduation rates of African American youth in North Omaha. Underscoring former Senator Council's argument during a 1985 legislative hearing addressing the re-industrialization of North Omaha, former Senator Chambers reminded his colleagues of the negative consequences of the North Freeway, stating that it did not promote economic development as promised, instead all it did was displace people from their homes, raise unemployment due to the loss of local businesses, and strengthen the control of outside interest over the area.

The destruction of the Black community in North Omaha can be measured in quantity and quality of life. *Omaha World-Herald* staff writer C. David Kotok (1983, p. 4A) reported, "during the '70s, the community survived on memories and sentiment as the city eliminated 700 houses and scattered 2,000 people to make way for the North Freeway." The "free" way has been very costly for Omaha's Black residents living on the Near North Side.

Perceptions of the North Freeway

Pastor Williams commented that people are still protesting the North Freeway. A recent protest came in the form of a $1 million business proposal titled "Demolish the North Freeway and Replace with an Urban Boulevard" and read:

> The North Freeway cut through much of North Omaha in the late 20th century against the wishes of the residents of the neighborhood and led to the demolition of

2,000 buildings in the neighborhood, cutting it in two. Originally intended to link up with I-680 past Florence, construction on it was stopped once it reached Florence, and now mainly exists as a little stub freeway with only three exits. Traffic data from the city of Omaha shows that it is underused as well. Furthermore, data shows that air quality around the North Freeway is lower than elsewhere in the city, leading to higher risks of asthma and COPD. A modern boulevard with good transit could easily carry the traffic currently handled by the North Freeway while taking up less space, allowing more space for transit-oriented affordable housing to spring up.

Pastor Williams felt that the North Freeway was detrimental to the community. He explained that he learned about the North Freeway within five or six years of arriving in Omaha. "I think it was devastating to people. It broke up communities. It did exactly what the White folks who did it wanted it to do. It broke up communities and created disunity and disorganization. Believe it or not, there are conversations about doing away with it." He continued uninhibited, "It's certainly a big negative for the community, and it was intended to be."

He continued, noting other cities in which the highway system was used to break up Black neighborhoods and communities. Describing a civil rights trip he takes high school students on annually, he shared,

> We were in Tulsa [Oklahoma] getting a tour from a resident, and I say we, so Preston, myself, and others, have been doing this tour for high school students for the last six years. We used to start in Memphis, then we started

going to Jackson, Birmingham, Montgomery, Selma, Tuskegee, and then to Atlanta. So, this year, we added Tulsa. So, we are in Tulsa, walking from the Tulsa Rising Museum down to the church where people hid during the riot in 1921 or the massacre, and there's an interstate there. The guy is telling us the story, but he's not talking about the interstate, so Preston interrupted him and said, "Everybody look! Just like in Omaha, there's this interstate that they put through the Black community."

Pastor Williams felt that city planners wanted to control and disrupt Black communities and used the transportation system to achieve their goals. He explained it as the "idea that we are going to break up your harmony. You've got too much harmony here." The economic and social devastation is readily visible when I drive through the Pratt Street neighborhood and the surrounding area split up by the North Freeway. It certainly did break up the harmony of my childhood community.

City planning and disinvestment

As Pastor Williams continued to discuss the impact of the North Freeway on the Black community, the conversation naturally segued into the economic impact of disinvestment in the area. He shared, "My friend Preston talks about the fact that there has been virtually no investment in North Omaha in 50 years. Those things speak to the mindset of people then and now, in my view."

Interviews conducted with city officials in 1983 by the staff of the *Omaha World-Herald* confirm Preston's observations and Pastor Williams' point about the mindset of city administrators and tell a story of deliberate neglect of the Near North Side. In an interview about the economic challenges facing the Near North Side since the 1950s, former City Planning Director Alden Aust admitted that "the city did little to stem the tide of deterioration during the 1960s and 1970s" and said, "As planning director, I knew the city should have done more, but the city councils and mayors of the 1960s and '70s refused to invest in the Near North Side because voters had turned thumbs down on urban renewal" (Kotok, 1983, p. 4-A).

The city's majority White voting population was not interested in seeing their tax dollars put to use in building up an area occupied primarily by Black low-income and working-class residents and previously ravished by riots in 1966, 1968, and 1969. In fact, former Mayor Eugene Leahy used the racial tensions existing at the time as an excuse for not doing more. He told the reporter that "the decline of the Near North Side was like an economic cancer in the community, [that] something should have been done, but under the tensions we suffered then, no one trusted anybody" (Kotok, 1983, p. 4-A).

Another excuse offered by city officials was that the city needed to gain experience with neighborhood redevelopment. Omaha's Planning and Community Development Director in the 1980s, Marty Shukert, told the *Omaha World-Herald* reporter that "in the mid-1970s, the city lacked the expertise to do much about neighborhood problems." So, instead, federal block grant funds were "poured into downtown development projects of the sort that had been accomplished through urban renewal programs in other cities," Shukert explained (Kotok, 1983, p. 4-A). However, Shukert pointed out that a neighborhood on the Near North Side was one of 13 neighborhoods that the city allotted federal funds to improve streets, sidewalks, and alleys. While necessary, these kinds of cosmetic improvements to an area play a minor role in strengthening the economic and social conditions of the community.

Black investment in Omaha

"It's the philanthropic community kind of controlling and determining when and what investments happen in the area," Pastor Williams observed. He felt that North Omaha would be better off with independent sources of economic development to reduce the dependency on philanthropists' funding. Reflecting on Black enterprise in North Omaha, he shared that Jews mostly owned the businesses in North Omaha because Black people have never had access to capital on a large scale to develop a significant Black economy in North Omaha. However, he hopes the ARPA (Federal American Rescue Plan Act) will fund more entrepreneurial opportunities for African Americans. Senators Terrell McKinney and Justin Wayne share Pastor Williams' hope for the ARPA funds. In a call to action letter included in the *North Omaha Recovery Plan 2022 – 2025*, they describe the ARPA dollars as "once in a lifetime" or "transformational funding to support North Omaha "recover from the social, public health, and economic impacts of COVID-19 and emerge more vibrant and resilient," (McKinney & Wayne, 2022, p.3). Reflecting on the small-scale of Black-owned businesses, he shared, "I think this is an area in America that has certainly not lived up to its promise." The long history of banks denying Black Americans access to residential and commercial capital has constrained and curtailed Black enterprise in Black communities for centuries.

Pastor Williams felt that perceptions and attitudes also fueled and exacerbated the problem. He shared,

> When the current Mayor [Jean Stothert] became mayor, within about five days of being elected, she came to North Omaha right down the street, talked to people about her perceptions and goals, and so forth. And her thought was to bring business in! She's going to bring business from other cities to Omaha! Well, what about growing your *own* business?!?! She's in North Omaha, and they don't even think that Black people are capable of being business owners. That's not even part of their perception. So, there's a problem there. We have to think more about businesses ourselves as well. So, I think it works both ways.

Redevelopment efforts

One of the ways that ARPA funds are being used in Omaha includes a $20 million partnership with Front Porch Investments (FPI), a non-profit organization supporting affordable housing development in historically disinvested and formerly redlined neighborhoods like North Omaha (Front Porch, n.d.). According to the City of Omaha Recovery Plan report, the Affordable Housing Program funds "will make new affordable housing units available, preserve and improve the quality of existing housing units, and increase opportunities for homeownership for low to moderate-income families" (City of Omaha, 2022 Recovery Plan Performance Report, p. 4).

Another promising redevelopment project involves a partnership with key organizations, community stakeholders, and city planners to revitalize North 24th Street. The project is known as the Forever North Omaha Project. According to its strategic planning document, it is a strategic action-oriented plan to develop the North 24th Street corridor "into a vibrant, livable community that values existing residents, attracts new community members, and offers opportunities and experiences everyone can enjoy" (Viero, 2021, p. 5). The key priorities of the approach emphasize the importance of attracting new residents and businesses without displacing existing community members and preserving and promoting the area's rich history, culture, and art.

It is encouraging to see that the stakeholder committee and community partners involved in the project include an extensive array of long-term North Omaha residents and organizations, including Mount Moriah Baptist Church's former pastor, Ralph Lassiter. The renovation and revitalization efforts of North 24th Street are underway and have been clearly visible during my numerous visits to Omaha.

Chapter 8
Berdine Hall Williams

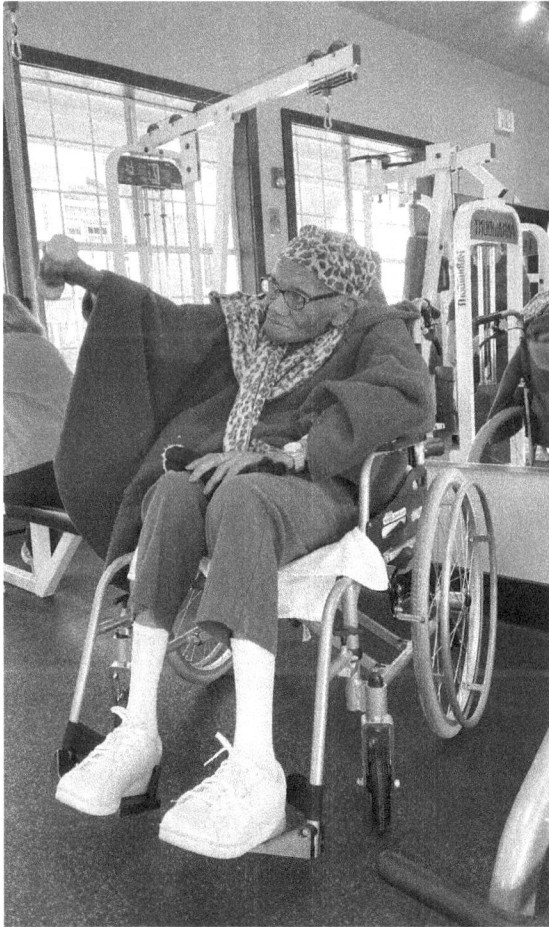

Berdine Williams staying fit in Fayetteville, Arkansas

Living and working in her 90s

I vividly remember leaving my grandparents' home the first time my family moved to another state. We were all piled up in our two-door white Ford Mercury Marauder headed to Alton, Illinois. It was 1965. Grandma was standing on the sidewalk near the back door of the Pratt Street house in her white nursing uniform, waving goodbye. I sat in the back seat of the car, bawling, thinking I would never see her or my grandpa again. I was devastated and vowed to myself that I would die before her so I wouldn't have to ever endure the pain of a broken heart from being separated from her again. I was five years old, with no idea that that would not be the last time I saw my grandparents, nor the last time I would leave them.

I grew accustomed to our military family moving to a different state every three years, but deep down I never got accustomed to having to say goodbye to my grandparents. I was able, fortunately, to spend most of my summers with them growing up. And we lived right next door to them between 1966 and 1968. We also visited them during Thanksgiving, Christmas, and Grandma's birthday, especially after she turned 90; Kinze started renting a stretch limousine for Grandma's birthday when she turned 90 and taking her and the family to the casino for all-you-can-eat buffets and a little bit of gambling. Grandma liked to play the nickel slot machines.

Every year we went to Omaha for Grandma's birthday after her 90th, there was this unspoken apprehension in the air that it might be her last birthday. No one would say it openly, but I think we all thought it. I guessed that family superstitions about openly saying someone might die is a step away from willing them to die is what prevented us from giving voice to our fears. Or perhaps, maybe, it was only me that harbored this fear. Besides, Grandma was in good health and still working with Aunt Doris, caring for vulnerable adults through the Faith, Hope, & Charity Corporation. They were also collectively raising Grandma's great-grandson, my third cousin, Michael, who was in high school by that time.

There was no reason, given these facts, to worry about how much longer Grandma had to live. But I worried just the same. Perhaps, deep down, my childhood self was feeling anxious, remembering the sadness of the first time I was separated from her as a five-year-old and wondering how I would live without her as an adult, given that childhood promise I made to myself. Grandma was getting close to 100 years old, and we had no experience with anyone in the family who had lived that long. What we did have, though, was years of watching her take care of older adults, which provided me with some assurance that our family could care for her whenever the occasion arose. She was still living independently, although Michael lived with her, and Aunt Doris was right next door and could check on her if needed.

When Grandma turned 90, she started telling people her age. Surprised by this, I asked her about it. Laughing, she retorted, without hesitation, "Because, honey, 90 is something to talk about!" A month after her birthday, in April 2009, she received "The Shirley Waskel Award for Women's Advancement" from the University of Nebraska-Omaha Lifelong Learning Initiative's Program for Women and Successful Aging. Her family traveled from around the country to witness her honor at the 5th Annual

Women of Wisdom Award luncheon held at the Holiday Inn Central on South 72nd Street.

Grandma sat dignified for photos at the luncheon, her silver hair framing her beautiful mocha brown face, reflected in the shiny silver inscribed award plate that she cradled in her hands. Her three daughters, Ida, Bobbie Jean, and Doris stood behind her for the photo, and her son Kinze knelt by her side. The only one physically missing from the picture was Grandpa, and I was sure he was there, in spirit, on her other side. I imagined him in his grey-blue herringbone tweed suit and Fedora with a soft smile beaming across his face. I could see him holding Grandma's hand, squeezing it ever so slightly just to let her know he had her back as he had in life. My heart swelled with pride as I watched her, surrounded by her loved ones. Ironically, I was walking with the use of a cane at that time, having had major surgery, while Grandma was vibrantly waltzing around the banquet hall, greeting the other award recipients and dignitaries who attended.

Grandma was a lifelong learner and took her religious study as seriously as her nursing vocation. She and Aunt Doris attended Mount Nebo Missionary Baptist Church's month-long Bible study class for their religious teaching certification. Grandma was the oldest student in the class, at 98 years old, to receive the certificate.

In June 2010, a few months after her 91st birthday, Grandma was admitted to Bergan Mercy Hospital and diagnosed with pneumonia and Chronic Obstructive Pulmonary Disease (COPD). As she started recovering, the doctor wanted to release her, but she did not feel she was healed enough to go home, so her personal doctor convinced the hospital to let her stay inpatient for a little over a month. While she was continuing to recuperate, the nurses at the hospital constantly tried to persuade her to consider convalescing in a nursing home. Aunt Doris explained, "Momma did not want to go into a nursing home. I had to contact the director of nurses at the hospital and tell her the nurses were harassing Momma and that they needed to stop because they were upsetting her. That affected her healing." After she was released from the hospital, the family decided that it would be best for Grandma to live with Aunt Doris, and she and Uncle Kenzie helped her recover completely.

It was the first time I saw Grandma sick. She sat in her nightgown most of the day, hooked up to a heavy green metal oxygen tank supported by two small wheels that made it easier to roll around. I trembled inside with the fear that I would not survive if she died. She had become my saving grace, my Rock of Gibraltar. She was my internal "go-to" as I witnessed her steadfast faith throughout my life. A faith that escaped me. A faith in a God I struggled to embrace. I was not ready to lose her. I believed I would never be ready.

Aunt Doris said Grandma was motivated to get well. She did everything she needed to recover fully, and by the time of her 92nd birthday she was off the oxygen and ready for another limousine ride out to the casino for the all-you-can-eat buffet and slot machines. She was also back to providing semi-independent care to adults with Aunt Doris, which included preparing meals, supervising medications, and arranging transportation.

Grandma decided not to renew her driver's license in her early 90s. Aunt Doris recalled, "I was thankful that Momma voluntarily decided to stop driving. She told me that she has a clean driving record with no accidents or tickets and wants to keep it that way." Although Grandma lived with Aunt Doris, it was not uncommon for her to go to her own house next door to do her laundry, look through her mail, and cook. My Mom had bought her a new washer, dryer, and stove, and she enjoyed using these appliances whenever possible. In 2014, for Grandma's 95th birthday, her children, grandchildren, and great-grandchildren gathered in Omaha to celebrate. She had lost some weight during her illness, and she looked like she had lost another inch or two in height. Her hair was grayer, but her spirit was high, and she was happy to see us. And I was so glad to see her too.

This birthday was special because my older brother James and his daughter Larissa, from California, attended the celebration. James had not been to Omaha since Grandpa died 20 years earlier. My seven-year-old niece, Larissa, was meeting her great-grandmother for the first time, having only seen her in photos and talked with her on the phone. During a visit to California years earlier, Grandma and Grandpa met Skylar and Ryan, James' sons, when they were little boys. "Come here, honey, and give your great grandma some sugar!" Grandma said as she stretched her arms out to hug Larissa.

Very shy at first, Larissa inched toward Grandma. Grandma enveloped her with a long, warm embrace as she kissed Larissa on the cheek. It took Larissa a minute to warm up to her great-grandmother. She frequently peeked at her father and Grandma

Ida, looking for their guidance on how to respond to the numerous compliments Grandma showered on her about being a good girl and the many questions that followed. Grandma asked her about how she liked school, her favorite subjects and things to do, her friends, and so on. After a short while, it was clear from her animated responses and facial expressions that Larissa was more relaxed and enjoying telling Grandma different things about her life in California. At some point, Larissa fell into playing with her cousins as the novelty of meeting her great-grandmother subsided.

Grandma then turned her attention to James, calling him by his nickname after another warm embrace. "Chubby, it's so good to see you again. How long has it been? I'm sure glad you could make it for my birthday and bring my sweet great-granddaughter to meet me. How are those boys of yours doing? They must be grown by now." After catching up on everyone's lives, we settled into a delicious dinner. We watched Grandma open her presents and read all her birthday cards aloud to us as she savored the attention and love surrounding her. We took as many photos as possible of James and Larissa with Grandma in addition to the family photos we typically took at her birthday celebrations. We commemorated Grandma's 95th birthday with lovely 20-page professional photo album books produced by Monie.

The front cover of the baby blue photo album features a picture of Grandma wearing beige slacks and a long-sleeve grey shirt with the word 'Arkansas' in red across the chest and her signature leopardskin felt hat adorning her head. The Arkansas shirt was given to me as a gift for Grandma the year before, in 2013, by the University of Arkansas when I was hired as a tenure-track assistant professor in the School of Social Work and African and African American Studies. When I told Grandma that the University of Arkansas offered me a job, the first thing she asked me was, "Honey, do they know you are Black?" She shared her concern: "My state better take good care of my first granddaughter." I reminded her regularly that I was doing fine in Arkansas. The back cover of the photo album has a photograph of Grandpa's headstone, and below it, "Always in our hearts and with us in spirit is Mr. Bobby Williams, Mr. Nelson Williams, and Ms. Bobbie Jean Williams." Grandma loved the photo album, as did we.

The fall and surgery

On March 8, 2019, 16 days before her 100th birthday, Grandma fell on the sidewalk outside of Aunt Doris' house and fractured her right hip. She had to have surgery and a rod placed in her hip at Bergan Mercy Medical Center. She was in the medical center for four days and transferred on March 12 to the CHI Health Immanuel Fontenelle Rehabilitation Institute for two months. While she was in the medical center, I set up a schedule for a family member to stay in her room with her continuously while she recuperated from the surgery. I also purchased her an iPod and recorded her favorite gospel music to provide her spiritual comfort as she healed. Her pastor at the time, Reverend Ralph Lassiter, and several members of Mount Moriah Baptist Church also visited her in the hospital, lifting her spirits. I could see in her eyes that she was happy to see them.

After her surgery, Grandma mostly slept. But not restfully. I sat in the reclining chair at the foot of her bed, watching her sleep. She was propped up partially by pillows in a blue hospital gown and matching hair net. I could see from her furrowed brow and pursed lips that she was in pain. A clear plastic oxygen tube loosely secured in her nose, wrapped around her ears, and attached to a tube below her neck added to the strain I witnessed on her face. Three hospital bracelets, red, blue, and yellow, adorned her right arm, and an intravenous (IV) line was taped to the back of her right hand. I reminded myself, overcome by emotions of helplessness, that the medical accoutrements attached to her face and body were to facilitate healing. Nevertheless, it was unsettling to see her lying there, so vulnerable and in pain. I consoled myself with the hope that the gospel music coming through her headphones offered her a modicum of comfort.

As she continued to recover, Grandma started asking regularly when she could go home. The doctors and nurses kept reminding her that she would need to spend time at the rehabilitation center before she could return home. It was obvious that Grandma did not want to stay in the hospital a minute longer than she needed to be there. While it was certainly understandable that she wanted to go home, I was relieved that the doctors seemed to err on the side of caution and did not show any signs that she should be discharged prematurely.

When she was transferred by ambulance to the Immanuel Fontenelle Rehabilitation Institute, Grandma was assigned to room 148A on a virtually deserted wing of the facility far away from the nurse's station. After she was settled in the bed, the care attendants entered the room, took care of her bandaged hip, gave her some medicine, went over her care plan, and left. That was the last time anyone came into her room that evening.

I stayed with her all night; it was a night from hell that I felt would never end.

Grandma wanted to go home, and no matter how I tried to explain that she had to stay there until she could walk again, it did not stop her from calling out the names of everyone in the family to get her. At some point, I thought it might be helpful for her to talk to some family and friends. When I called Jendayi, she told her, "I want to go home, and Tina won't let me out of here," calling me by my nickname. She continued, "I can't believe that my own granddaughter would treat me this way. I didn't raise her to be like this. Honey, come and get me out of here!" Everyone I called tried to console her as well, to no avail. It was hard to hear Grandma say that I was mistreating her because I would never do that, and I wanted to help her in every way that I could. She was right about raising me to respect my elders. I had to balance my feelings with the facts and stay focused on trying to relieve her suffering.

At some point, to my surprise and alarm, despite having had surgery only four days earlier, she tried to slide out of the bed like she was planning on walking out of the room. I wondered what kind of pain medication they had given her since she was not complaining about being in physical pain or even wincing when she moved. I guessed her amygdala had kicked into overdrive and was in fight mode. Her stamina and determination were unbelievable!

Exhausted and confused, I pushed the call button for someone from the facility to assist, but no one ever came. I pulled the couch in the corner of the room closer to Grandma's bed, held her hand, and told her, "Grandma, I am here with you. You are not alone." I tried to calm her and keep her from getting out of bed. My efforts did not calm her, but they did stop her from attempting to get up. "Would you like to listen to your gospel music? "I asked pleadingly. "No! I want to go home!" she shot back at me. I knew it was going to be a long night after that response. We were up all night.

The following morning, I was exhausted, frustrated, and quite irritable when Aunt Doris informed me that she called the director of Immanuel and told them what I had shared with her, that the staff never entered the room again after Grandma's initial intake assessment. Worn out by the long night, Grandma had finally settled into sleep. A supervisor entered the room and verified that Grandma had not received additional care on her first night there. They moved her to a different room nearer a nurse's station and a wing with more residents in the facility. I was not confident that this change would make any difference in her care after the disappearing act I witnessed from the staff the night before.

I decided to make another schedule for family members and friends to stay with Grandma every day and night while she was at the rehab center. We took turns to ensure that she was with one of us in the morning, afternoon, evening, and night and would never be left alone. Having someone with her at all times was also a way of holding the rehab center accountable. We told the staff that regardless of their visiting hours, Grandma would always have a family member or friend present with her.

Most family and friends lived in Omaha; however, my companion, RoAnne, and I had to travel from Arkansas when we were scheduled to stay with Grandma. Thankfully, Immanuel had a partnership with a nearby hotel to give family and friends visiting their loved ones for an extended period a discount on the hotel room rates. This allowed us more flexibility and enabled us to visit with Grandma at times before or after our scheduled shifts. It also provided us with a space for much-needed respite. I could stay in Omaha for a few days and help Aunt Doris shop for Grandma, do her laundry, and bring in foods she liked to eat. She enjoyed chicken and dumpling soup and fried chicken, besides the food on the Immanuel menu.

Rehabilitation

Grandma played an active role in how she was cared for at Immanuel. She did not hesitate to let a nurse, certified nursing aid (CNA), or technician know if she was in pain when they were moving her or if she needed assistance that was not forthcoming. Equally, she was quick to praise their efforts and let them know she appreciated them. I assumed that because she had spent most of her life providing nursing care for others, she knew what to expect and what kind of care most benefited her. Most of the staff became accustomed to hearing her share her observations and sometimes offering direction regarding her needs. There was a fine line between telling them how to do their jobs and how to meet her specific needs. I guess at 99 years old, Grandma figured she had earned the right to be direct and explicit about her care. The staff were professional and attentive most of the time after that first night.

A significant part of Grandma's recovery involved physical therapy (PT). Every morning after breakfast, the staff would wheel her into the physical therapy room to learn how to walk again. She enjoyed talking with the staff about her life and her family and learning about them. All of the PT staff were White, and one day, while they were talking with Grandma, she told them, "I didn't think I would ever see the day when White people would be waiting on me hand and foot." They took her comment in stride, while I thought she had to wait 100 years to have such an experience. One hundred years before she could be waited on by White people the way she had been waiting on them a good portion of her life. I sat there quietly, trying not to let my emotions overtake me as I felt the weight of her words sink in fully. She named a century of racial injustice with that one observation.

The staff had her doing strengthening exercises, stretches, and balancing work, and she slowly built up to walking again with the assistance of a walker. She sometimes joked with them about her age, telling them, "I'm 100 years old, you know, so don't forget that, honey, when you are setting up my activities. I'm no spring chicken like you all," she would say laughing. Another time, a resident she had befriended was joking with Grandma, telling her, "Mrs. Williams, you are walking kind of slow there." Grandma paused, looked at the resident, and wisecracked teasingly, "And how old are you?" Everyone around them burst into laughter. Grandma embraced her centenarian status with pride and was determined and motivated to heal. I marveled at her drive and perseverance as we videotaped her walking with the walker during PT and encouraged her verbally with each step she took to affirm her efforts. Often, Grandma pushed herself to take a few more steps beyond the number asked of her.

There were times when she felt discouraged and disappointed by what felt to her like slow progress. During these times, we would affirm her feelings, ask her if she wanted to listen to her gospel music, as it was a source of comfort for her most of the time, and show her the videotapes of herself walking to remind her that, although the recovery was slow, she was making progress. Grandma also joined the other residents at the church services held in the chapel on the premises a few times.

Celebrating 100 years

Despite the last-minute location change, I was overjoyed to see everyone who came to Grandma's 100th birthday party. Originally planned to take place at Mount Moriah Baptist Church, the celebration was moved to Immanuel because Grandma was still receiving rehabilitation services. The administrative staff graciously designated one of the unused wings of the building, clearing out the old equipment and setting up tables for us to use for the party. It worked out perfectly. There were roughly 40 people in attendance. In addition to all her family and friends, many members and pastors of her church, her family doctor, and friends of our friends joined us to witness, honor, and celebrate Grandma's resilience, wisdom, and remarkable life achievements.

My cousin Berdine, "Berdie," Grandma's namesake, did a fantastic job decorating the space primarily in blue, Grandma's favorite color, and white with splashes of silver and gold to distinguish this extraordinary milestone birthday. The tables were draped in royal blue tablecloths, each with a beautifully decorated floral centerpiece. Silver streamers and bunches of blue, white, and silver balloons adorned the room, adding flair to the festive atmosphere. There were several tables full of Grandma's favorite foods: chicken, fish, and turkey, as well as rice, potatoes, salads, and others. A full-size double-layered white marble sheet cake trimmed in blue and pink with a sparkling silver "100" cake topper set the stage for a beautiful celebration, along with the variety of brightly colored helium balloons scattered around the space.

The formal birthday presentations began with an opening prayer from Grandma's pastor, Reverend Lassiter, after dinner. Grandma's children honored her first, followed by several nieces, nephews, church members, and grandchildren. Grandma sat quietly, attentive in her sparkling gold floral patterned pantsuit and matching scarf, absorbing all the sights and sounds surrounding her. I wondered what was going through her mind as each person spoke about her significance in their lives and how special it was for them to celebrate her life. Grandma also received a beautiful letter of recognition from former Secretary of State Condoleezza Rice, whom she met in Washington, DC, in 2004 when Jendayi was sworn in as the US Ambassador to South Africa:

> Dear Mrs. Williams, Congratulations on your milestone birthday. You have been a model and an inspiration to generations—and now we have a chance to say thank you—and to wish you many more years of working to do the Lord's will. I love your motto that you will retire only when God retires you. I am sure that He still has plans for you.

> As a nurse and businesswoman, you overcame so many obstacles that history and circumstances put in your

path. But overcome them you did—and with a grateful spirit and joyousness that was infectious to all around you. You were never focused on yourself—but on those in need and thus helped so many receive quality health care and with it—hope. Mt. Moriah Missionary Church has been a second home to you and a great spiritual anchor. You have gone out from your church home to be a servant leader and a giver of compassion—just as the Lord commanded.

I know too your wonderful family and how you influenced your grandchildren and children. Your granddaughter Jendayi was my student at Stanford and has had an incredible career in government and academia. She often said that you were a model for her of how to use one's talents to help others.

So, on this, your 100th birthday, I just want to say thank you. I loved meeting you many years ago, and I hope our paths will cross again. Until then—God Bless You, and Happy Birthday.

The Honorable Karen Bass of the 37th Congressional District of California in the House of Representatives honored Grandma's 100th birthday in the first session of the Proceedings and Debates of the 116th Congress with, "Madam Speaker, on March 24, 2019, Mrs. Berdine Hall Williams will celebrate her 100th birthday. I congratulate her on her long life and many accomplishments, and I congratulate her family and friends on maintaining the connections with her that make a long life rich and rewarding." The recorded proceedings include a chronicle of Grandma's life and accomplishments.

We hired a professional photographer who did a great job documenting Grandma's celebration, and Mom made her a beautiful photo album to mark the event. We spent the whole afternoon and early evening commemorating Grandma. She gave a speech of gratitude and appreciation, thanking everyone for their presence in helping her celebrate her birthday.

As I reflected on the day, I thought about all that Grandma has survived in her 100 years on earth and the recent challenges that have come with a fractured hip, surgery, and rehabilitation. While she is vibrant and engaged for a 100-year-old woman, she is vulnerable and dependent on the will and kindness of others to get her basic needs met. While I know that no one is entirely self-sufficient, watching Grandma makes me understand helplessness and dependency in a new way. Being with her made me think more seriously about how I am living my life now and what I give priority to, take for granted, and see as serious or frivolous. Witnessing her life helped me reevaluate what is important and how I want to use my short time on this earth. I want to be more intentional about my life and really do the work necessary to create the life I want to live. She is my inspiration.

Assisted living

When Grandma was discharged from Immanuel, she could not return to Aunt Doris' house because it was not set up for using a walker. Jendayi made it financially possible for Grandma and Aunt Doris to move into an independent living two-bedroom apartment at the Pacific Springs Village, an upscale retirement community located in the wealthy White region of West Omaha. Jendayi also hired two independent CNAs, Javon and Mylina, to help care for Grandma. My university allowed me a modified work arrangement to work in Arkansas and Omaha. I rented a one-bedroom apartment above Grandma and Aunt Doris to help care for Grandma and take her to church on Sundays and any appointments. I created another schedule and care plan that included Grandma's loved ones to ensure that she had around-the-clock care every day:

Care plan for Berdine Williams

1. **Attentiveness**—always speak respectfully to Berdine, exercising patience and gentleness in tone and attitude. Answer any questions she may have about anything, no matter how often she asks the same questions.

2. **Independence**—always allow Berdine to lead the way, doing as much as she can independently of you, but be ready to support her as she needs it and requests specific support.

3. **Asking for help**—always ask for help when you need it. For Berdine's safety, recognize your need for help and ask for it.

4. **Other care team members**—please recognize that several caregivers support Berdine's well-being. This will require coordination, communication, and cooperation on everyone's part. The Visiting Nurses Assoc. provides nursing, occupational therapy, physical therapy, and social work services over a 6–8-week period 2xs per week.

5. **Encouragement**—Berdine responds well to verbal encouragement and praise for her efforts in using her walker and exercising. It helps her to hear "good job, A+" while demonstrating your support with a thumbs up or clapping your hands, for example, to encourage her.

Grandma used her walker well in her new apartment and continued receiving PT. Still, the surroundings were unfamiliar to her, and she was now living in an exclusively White community. As we moved about the environment, taking her to the dining room for dinner, outside for a stroll around the facilities, or to lounge in areas designated for socializing, everyone we saw was White. Everyone was friendly and welcoming and did their best to help us acclimate to the new living space.

Grandma was beginning to show signs of memory loss, and Javon and Mylina came up with the idea of getting a whiteboard on which we wrote messages for Grandma to read to help answer some of the regular questions she would ask. For example, the board might read: *Today is Thursday, September 19, 2019. This is your house. Jendayi bought it for you. You live here with your daughter Doris*. We also put on the board that *you live in a nice neighborhood with very friendly neighbors who are kind to each other and their children, grandchildren, nieces, and nephews*. Eventually, the board became a critical communication tool for keeping all of Grandma's caregivers updated and informed about things happening in the environment relevant to her care and of importance to her. The board's content also typically included a spiritually uplifting message or scripture. Grandma read the board regularly, and when I was in Arkansas and talking to her over the phone, frequently she would read the board to me.

Michael was scheduled to assist Grandma, typically during the night shift. She often worried about him, as a young Black man, coming into a White neighborhood late at night and leaving early in the morning when fewer people were moving around.

We had to reassure her constantly that he was safe from harm. We did this in several ways. We put on the board that *Michael is at work. He will be here at 7 pm to spend the night with you. JA will be here with you until 7 pm.* After Michael left in the morning, he would Facetime with Grandma to let her know he had arrived safely home. Michael also made a videotaped recording of himself talking to Grandma about what he was doing and where he was. We played the video for her when she asked about him throughout the day.

In October 2019, Grandma had to have a procedure done to open the arteries in her legs to increase the blood flow to her feet. She underwent the procedure on her left leg first and, two weeks later, the right leg. She was sedated both times and recovered well. Witnessing her resilience, resolve, and faith was amazing as she was informed about the procedures and prepped, and her recovery afterward was amazing. She asked critical questions about the process and what she could expect and put her trust in God like she always did to see her through.

We used the whiteboard extensively to help her remember why she had to go to the "foot doctor" and "the procedure" she was having and why. She had memories of going to the foot doctor in the past, and we decided to use the phrase "procedure" instead of "surgery" to reduce her anxiety. During Grandma's follow-up appointment four months later, her doctor tested the circulation in her legs and the pulse in her feet and said all the tests came back showing good circulation and a solid, strong pulse. She rejoiced at the good news, as did we, and thanked God. Grandma continued to make progress using the walker, too. Shinaye, Grandma's granddaughter, came up with the idea of lacing the walker with a string of bells because Grandma would get up in the middle of the night and walk to the bathroom sometimes without assistance, even though one of us always slept in her bedroom to assist her throughout the night if needed.

Visiting a dear friend

One Sunday, at church, Grandma was told that her lifelong friend Mrs. Lampkin was dying. They had celebrated their birthdays together many years since they were less than a week apart. When Mrs. Lampkin was diagnosed with Alzheimer's, Grandma started visiting her during their birthdays in the facility she was living in for a while until Mrs. Lampkin was moved back with her family. Grandma kept asking to see Mrs. Lampkin after hearing at church that she was not doing well. Javon wrote on the board: *Tina is in Arkansas. Michael is at work. We will see Mrs. Lampkin when her daughter calls to let us know it is okay. Remember, God loves us all.* After reading the board aloud, Grandma said, "You ain't got to tell me about God. I know Him for myself."

I contacted Mrs. Lampkin's daughter, hoping that Grandma could visit her only remaining peer since she had outlived all her friends in her age cohort. "I can only imagine that this is a difficult time for your family," I said, trying to demonstrate compassion and respect. "I am reaching out with the hope that you will receive this with my intention to respect your family's privacy and, simultaneously, respond to my Grandma's request to see her dearest friend," I continued. I explained that Grandma was 100 years old now, but she remembered Mrs. Lampkin and wanted to say goodbye to her if she could as her only remaining long-term friend. Her daughter was very welcoming of Grandma coming for a visit. She explained that her mother was not eating much and was unable to open her eyes, so she was not sure how much longer she would live.

Since I was in Arkansas then, I contacted Javon and asked her to let Grandma know that I was heading back to Omaha in the morning and could take her to see her friend. When Javon told Grandma she would have to wait until I arrived, Grandma responded impatiently, "Weight is what broke the bridge," and that she was going to get in her car and go on her own to see Mrs. Lampkin. She was upset the remainder of the day, and when I arrived, she said, "Tina, let's go. I want to see my friend before she dies." On the way over to the family's house, Grandma asked me, "Does Bessie know we are coming? How do I look? I wonder if she will recognize me?" I reassured her that she looked fine and reminded her that Mrs. Lampkin's health was declining, so we could not be sure if she would recognize her until we arrived. Grandma responded, "Maybe I should let my hair down. Bessie remembers me with long hair, and I will have to tell her that my hair fell out as I got old." Grandma pulled her gray curls down so Mrs. Lampkin would recognize her.

I reassured Grandma that the family knew we were on our way, but I did not share what her daughter told me about her inability to eat or open her eyes. I also did not tell Grandma that Mrs. Lampkin was receiving hospice care and on a morphine drip. Grandma wanted to put on eyeliner and lipstick to look her best, but when Mylina offered to help her with it, she changed her mind. When she got in the car, she looked disappointedly in the mirror and said, "I don't have on eyeliner, lipstick, nothing," a bit deflated. Then she looked at herself again and said, 'Lampkin's will just have to see me like I came into this world." She had forgotten that Mrs. Lampkin was dying, so I reminded her again that she would likely not be able to talk. Grandma wanted to know, "What's wrong with her? Is she at her house? Where's her son and daughter?" I would remind her that we were going to see her at her son's house, not at Mrs. Lampkin's house.

Grandma talked all the way to the house, remembering what she and Mrs. Lampkin did when she first moved to the Pratt Street neighborhood in 1952. Mrs. Lampkin lived down the street and used to help with the patients in her residential care home. Grandma remembered Mrs. Lampkin's husband and how nice and helpful they were to her and Grandpa. She recalled how Mr. Lampkin had rounded up his buddies to donate blood to the Red Cross when Monie was born in 1966 and needed a complete blood transfusion.

Once inside the house, Grandma sat in the chair next to Mrs. Lampkin's bed. Mrs. Lampkin had her head turned toward the window opposite Grandma's chair. Grandma reached over and gently shook her on the shoulder, saying, "Bessie, this is Mrs. Williams. How are you? Open your eyes, talk to me." No response. Grandma shook her shoulder again and then patted her head, urging her "to say something." Mrs. Lampkin opened her eyes but could not turn her head toward Grandma.

Grandma kept talking to her and urging her to talk. Mrs. Lampkin moved her mouth but could not get any words out. Grandma was distressed at witnessing her friend in this condition and said, "She doesn't know it's me." I reassured her that Mrs. Lampkin did know it was her because she opened her eyes. Grandma did not seem too reassured. She eventually stopped trying after a few more times. She said, "Lampkin is on her way to heaven, so we might as well leave." As we were leaving, I spoke with Mrs. Lampkin's daughter-in-law, briefly asking how she was holding up, and thanked her for allowing Grandma to come over to see her friend.

Grandma was silent for most of the ride on the drive back to the apartment. We stopped by her old neighborhood on Pratt Street, and she got to see Mrs. Lampkin's house, her niece Mrs. Ruby's house, and the lot on which her house used to stand. A couple of times, she said, "Mrs. Lampkin didn't know who I was," or "She is on her way to heaven." Two days after Grandma's visit, Mrs. Lampkin died, and Grandma was able to attend her wake and her funeral at Salem Baptist Church. At the wake, we wheeled Grandma up to the casket and took her walker. She stood up and talked to Mrs. Lampkin before returning to her chair. She sat through the whole funeral, looking at the program without saying too much. I was happy we could facilitate Grandma's visit with her last remaining friend and attend her homegoing.

Joy and gratitude

Grandma's board read, *Hi, today is Friday, August 23rd. This house belongs to you and Doris. Jendayi bought it for you. Michael is here now, and he will stay with you tonight. Please remember not to stand on your own for safety reasons. God is love!* This evening, after we returned to the apartment from our visit to the cemetery, Grandma started reading the whiteboard. After dinner, she returned to rereading it, and every time she finished, she would say, "I really enjoy reading the messages my grandchildren write to me." "I love my grandchildren, and I know they love me." "Ain't that a blessing?!"

Later, I had to return to work in the upstairs apartment, so I told Grandma I would call her in an hour to talk with her again. When I called her, the first thing she said was, "I'm glad you kept your promise. I like talking with my grandkids." I asked her what she was doing, and she told me she was reading her board. For over an hour, she read the board to me and told me how much she knows her grandchildren love her and how much she loves us. She told me that she loves reading the messages her grandchildren write for her on her board.

Every time she read that Jendayi bought the house for her and Doris, she would let out a celebratory "Hoo, hoo!" and say "How sweet that Jendayi is" or "Jendayi is killing us with kindness" or "Jendayi is such a blessing," or some other expression of joy and gratitude. We talked all night between her reading the board and telling me about the joy in her heart in knowing that her grandchildren loved her and the blessing in it all. I loved talking with Grandma and hearing the joy in her voice, and with every word we spoke, I could hear her smiling through the phone receiver. Her happiness reminded me of when Shinaye and Berdie were at the apartment caring for her, and they had fun laughing and watching movies all night.

We spent Thanksgiving and Christmas with Grandma while she and Aunt Doris lived at Pacific Springs Village. We had a traditional Thanksgiving feast with a big turkey, dressing, and several tasty side dishes. We put up a Christmas tree and lights, and family and friends traveled to Omaha to spend as much time as possible with Grandma and to encourage her as she gained skills in using the walker. We had a wonderful time sharing stories of significant milestones in our lives and enjoying the richness of family connections.

Returning to Arkansas

When Grandma left Arkansas in 1944 at the age of 25, although she had a constitutional right to vote, Jim Crow laws, poll taxes, literacy tests, and other voter suppression tactics used by the White power structure made it virtually impossible for Black people to exercise their legal right to cast a ballot for decades. Those who attempted to vote ran the risk of white violence and losing their lives, and many did. By the passage of the Voting Rights Act of 1965, Grandma was living in Omaha. Therefore, the first and last time she became a registered voter and voted in Arkansas, her birthplace, was in 2020 when she was 101 years old.

At some point, it became too challenging to coordinate Grandma's care in Omaha. RoAnne and I drove to Omaha, got Grandma, and brought her to Arkansas to live with me. We knew I would need assistance in caring for her. On the way to Omaha, RoAnne contacted several social service agencies to set up services for Grandma's care. On the drive back, we listened to Grandma's favorite gospel music, and she sat back, relaxed, and enjoyed the drive. I was worried about how her 100-year-old body would manage a six-hour car ride, but she did great. She enjoyed singing her favorite songs, talking, and napping at times.

The following day, after our arrival, Arkansas Hospice brought over a hospital bed and other equipment, and we set up a CNA service for Grandma through BrightStarCare. Hospice services are about end-of-life care. However, in my experience with the in-home hospice team that we worked with, the focus was on quality of life and living fully. They listened attentively to Grandma's needs and tailored their services as necessary to ensure the best support for her and us as her primary caregivers. I learned so much from Grandma and the hospice team about how to take care of her and ensure her quality of life and safety were at the forefront of every decision we made.

Much to my surprise and alarm initially, Grandma slept 12 to 14 hours straight the first few days after we came back to Fayetteville. I checked on her throughout her extended sleep patterns and tried to ease her transition as she acclimated to her new environment. We developed a structure of routines to create consistency and uniformity of care for Grandma and reinstituted the use of the whiteboard. For a while, my primary guide, beyond ensuring that her medical and PT needs were consistently met, was Grandma herself. She slept as long as she wanted, ate when and what she wanted, and told me, RoAnne, and the CNAs what she wanted and did not want to do.

Essentially, we followed Grandma's lead as long as it was safe. I figured that at 100 years old and principally in good health, she more than earned the right to do what she pleased whenever she wanted. One of the changes we instituted, at Grandma's request, was turning on her gospel music so that we all could enjoy it, so she stopped listening to it through her headphones. After a week or two of exclusively hearing gospel music, I decided to experiment a little with another genre of music that I like, jazz, to see how Grandma liked it.

I grew up watching her only listen to gospel music in her house; therefore, I was unsure how she would respond. She loved it! Her niece Ruby's son, Calvin Keyes, is an accomplished jazz guitarist and has produced many albums. I started with his music and told her she was listening to her grand-nephew. She loved that even more. She would bob her head, rock her feet, and clap her hands to the syncopated rhythms of Calvin's music just like she did her favorite gospel songs. At times, she would even request his music instead of the gospel! And it gave her bragging rights with the CNAs as she proudly let them know that they were listening to the music of her grand-nephew, Calvin. I also loved music that might be categorized as easy listening or elevator music. I tried it out one day, and Grandma hated it. She said, "What's that lousy music we are listening to now?" as we all laughed! Since that day, that genre of music has been dubbed "lousy music," whenever we hear it, or I play my "lousy music" playlists, we think of Grandma.

Another change we instituted happened gradually as Grandma would ask for things to eat and drink that she previously had not. For example, when I was growing up, she referred to pork as the devil's meat, and I never saw her eat it. However, once in a while, when she was in the rehabilitation center, she would have bacon with her breakfast. I thought it was a fad related to her environment, but she started asking for bacon at my house. We purchased turkey bacon, and she did not care for it much, so we got the real deal. Sometimes, she would have bacon with her breakfast and coffee. She was not a coffee drinker during my childhood, but she loved it, and so, with some mildly instituted limits, she ate anything she requested. A favorite dessert she liked was peach cobbler with vanilla ice cream, and Patti LaBelle's peach cobblers from Walmart were the best! We also made frequent trips to Dairy Queen for soft-serve ice cream like we used to get in Omaha on 30th Street when I was a child.

Building a new community

Living with my extraverted 100-year-old Grandma was like how I imagined it would be to live with a celebrity. She was a showstopper. People wanted to talk to her and paint her portrait; she got so much attention no matter where we went. My friends came over to meet and visit with her, and before the Covid-19 pandemic lockdown we had fun doing a lot of activities together outside the house. Grandma joined our exercise class and enjoyed chicken and dumpling lunches at the Olive Garden and shopping at Walmart. One day, our friends Anne Shelley and her partner Bridget Gibson came to the house to visit Grandma and had fellowship, listening to gospel music, testifying, witnessing, and praising the Lord. It was an uplifting and spiritually enriching gathering for us all, and Grandma talked about it often, saying, "It's just what my soul needed. Thank you, Jesus." It reminded me of my childhood and how important it was for the patients in Grandma's residential care home to have worship service in the house on Sundays when they could not go to church.

We also went for walks at Lake Fayetteville, a white space, and sat in the park people-watching. Inevitably, someone would start a conversation with Grandma, almost as if the rest of us were invisible. One time, we were pushing Grandma in her wheelchair on the walking path, and a group of guys were sitting out on the grass. One guy yelled to us, "I love what you are doing with your mother," as he pointed to Grandma. RoAnne and I looked at one another, puzzled, not understanding what he thought we were doing with Grandma beyond going for a stroll in the park. While I found the comment odd, I nodded and smiled in their direction to indicate that I heard him as we continued our walk.

Another time, when we were walking around the same lake with Grandma, a couple wanted to take a picture of us all. That was beyond weird, and I said, "No." I wondered why these White people were making such a big deal out of the ordinary things we were doing at the park. Like any other family, we were enjoying the fresh outdoor air and scenery around the lake with loved ones. I wondered if the virus had a deleterious effect on their brains and judgment. The hyper-visibility we experienced at those times was annoying and intrusive to me. I felt like we had become White people's scenery, spectacle, or entertainment. However, I did not let it ruin my time with my loved ones. I know my struggle with this kind of attention from White people when doing ordinary things is anchored in my lifelong experience of being racialized by a White dominant society.

Special events

As Grandma continued to acclimate to her new living space, the sunroom became one of her favorite spots in the house. Surrounded by windows, the sun shone through all day, providing a warm glow to the space. Grandma had a big, nice, cozy chair that not only reclined but lifted her to a standing position, making it much easier to help her transfer from the chair to use the walker. We assembled in the sunroom more than any other space in the house, and she started calling it the parlor. We decided to have Grandma's 101st birthday celebration in the parlor. By mid-March 2020, Covid-19 was in full swing, and so was mask-wearing. Therefore, most of the family did not travel then, but Mom flew in from California for Grandma's birthday celebration.

RoAnne ordered a beautifully decorated round cake with white icing topped with orange and white flowers and three blue-trimmed white candles with the number 101 and the inscription "Happy 101st birthday, Berdine!" We adorned the parlor with blue and white streamers and balloons and hung a "Happy 101 Birthday" banner over one of the windows. Grandma was elegantly dressed in her white pearl-beaded sweater and three-strand white pearl necklace. She wore a shiny silver tiara and lipstick that added to her radiance. So many flower arrangements were delivered for Grandma that we hardly had room for them and all the birthday cards she received!

This time, for the first time, I read Grandma's birthday cards to her as she smiled and shook her head, approving of the sentiments expressed. She was showered with cards from her grandchildren telling her, "You're celebrated today because to know you is to love you … and to love you is to be especially blessed!" Birthday cards from her children reminded her that she is "a gift from the Lord," "the kind of woman who brightens up the room," and told her "how much you are thought of and loved." She received cards from her nephew and nieces wishing her "all the joy your heart can hold, all the smiles a day can bring, every blessing that life can unfold, and God's gift of His best in everything." Grandma was overwhelmed with joy and gratitude as she listened and took in all the messages of love she received. We had fun eating, listening to Calvin's jazz, and listening to stories Grandma shared about her life with Grandpa when they were a young couple just starting a family together. Many of the family and friends in Omaha called or video chatted with Grandma with birthday wishes that added to a beautiful celebration.

Family visits and Grandparents' Day

Grandma started receiving more visitors from out of town as the country figured out how to travel safely during the pandemic. A family friend, Richard Partee, visited from Omaha several times. He said he promised Grandpa that he would be available to support Grandma. He went to see her in the hospital when she had hip surgery. He visited her regularly in the rehabilitation center and assisted living facility in Omaha, and he drove to Arkansas three or four times to see her. She was always delighted to visit with him and hear about his family and updates on life in Omaha.

In early September 2020, Shinaye, Berdie, Michael, Mimi, and Aunt Doris drove to Arkansas to visit Grandma. She was glad to see them all. Berdie's fiancé, Daunte, joined them on the drive down and asked Grandma's permission to marry Berdie. It was beautiful to watch how he got down on his knees and looked up earnestly at Grandma as she sat in her wheelchair, showing deference and respect for her as our family matriarch. Grandma cupped his hands as she tenderly questioned whether he was a man of God and had a church home. Using her marriage as an example, Grandma also gently schooled him on how important it was to treat Berdie with kindness always and never go to bed cross with each other. She patted his hands as she talked, and he responded, "Yes, ma'am," to her every word.

They could only stay the weekend, and Grandma was very sad to see them go. She did not feel like eating or getting out of bed for a few days. I lay beside her and read her scriptures. We set up a music box in the bedroom so she could listen to her favorite gospel songs. The hospice chaplain also visited to pray with Grandma whenever she wanted. Eventually, her sadness waned, and she returned to being engaged. One evening, as she was preparing for bed, Grandma said, "So Berdie is getting married? Ain't that a blessing? Go on, Berdie! I can't wait to see that!" Unfortunately, Grandma died in November before Berdie's wedding the following summer, but I know she was there in spirit, proud of her namesake.

About a week and a half after the grandchildren left, Mom and Jendayi visited for several weeks, and, with RoAnne, we planned to celebrate Grandparents' Day. We invited Grandma's children, grandchildren, nieces, nephews, cousins, and friends to join us in the virtual celebration of Grandma. Everyone tuned in from around the country, representing six generations, some of whom had never met. We all introduced ourselves in relation to Grandma, from the oldest to the youngest, and it felt like the branches of our intergenerational family tree had come alive right before our eyes. Grandma gave a speech:

I'm thankful to God to have all my nieces and, nephews and cousins here to be with us this afternoon. It's always nice to have family members around you. I don't want to say too much, or I will get to crying. So, I want to thank God for all those who could come today and those who wanted to come but were unable. And I wish all of you a happy day. I love you all.

I invited our ancestors into the space to be with us and guide our intentions in honoring Grandma, and, in so doing, we also honored them.

Grandma transitioned peacefully in her sleep on November 28, 2020. She was the last and longest-living child of Dennis and Ida Henderson Hall's 13 children, having lived 101 years. She carried the stories of her mother, Ida, and grandmother, Willie Ann Rogers, to her children and grandchildren, just as Willie Ann carried the stories of her mother, Lizzie Spotsell Johnson, to her children and grandchildren.

Collectively, they passed 186 years of their words, deeds, and stories lovingly to their offspring, hoping to equip us with the knowledge and skills necessary to live courageously, with conviction, and commitment to amplify and extend Black life. And to counter the White world's mythology about us. Our ancestors provided a foundation for us, a launching place to carry forward the cultural traditions of hope, faith, healing, and activism. They carved out spaces and places for us to embrace our birthright to be creative, dream, and fulfill our deepest aspirations. I am a granddaughter six generations removed from the enslavement of my great-great-great-grandmother, Lizzie Spotsell Johnson. I am one of the inheritors of their stories with a sacred calling to lovingly honor and cherish their lives and memories as their love and wisdom continue to sustain us.

Conclusion

Jendayi Frazer
Inheritance and legacy

Whether they traveled from Arkansas, Oklahoma, New Mexico, or Bermuda, the lives of the individuals and families represented here tell a story of collective resilience, resistance, and reclamation of a community besieged. They, too, are the conveyers of their ancestor's dreams, cultivating, creating, and bringing forth success and achievement in familiar and innovative ways. Ways that build bridges and sow seeds for successive generations on the Near North Side and beyond. They have collectively nurtured and promoted what scholar Mitchell (2020, p. 3) calls "homemade citizenship." Mitchell defines homemade citizenship as the actions, words, gestures, and deeds Black Americans take to affirm their lives, succeed, and create a sense of belonging and community while simultaneously recognizing that their pursuits and achievements will garner White fear and a "know-your-place" backlash of violence. White violence can take many forms, including physical anti black attacks, segregation, disinvestment, and gentrification of Black families and communities. It can take the form of surveillance, mass incarceration, redlining, predatory lending practices, disenfranchisement, voter suppression, and redistricting legislation. The splitting up of Black communities through eminent domain and highway construction is also a form of White violence to keep Black people in their "proper" place.

When the Tarver family found a way to recreate a sense of community for themselves and their offspring after the city confiscated their home in North Omaha through eminent domain to build the North Freeway, they exercised homemade citizenship. When Pastor T. Michael Williams continues year after year to take high school students on civil rights trips and teach them the real history of America, he is enacting homemade citizenship. He was practicing homemade citizenship when he built a children's ministry in North Omaha. When Linda refused to let her employer deny her the economic security she needed to maintain her house for as long as she could and set her sons up for a stellar education and career path, she was manifesting homemade citizenship. And when our grandparents focused on acquiring the homes and land they needed to build a thriving residential center and nursing home that served the North Omaha community for nearly 40 years, despite a history of redlining and housing segregation, they also practiced homemade citizenship.

Remembering our grandparent's 2801 Pratt Street house, Jendayi said, "I had fun growing up there." She believes fundamentally that "a child's sense of what is possible is based on what their parents and relatives have done." She continued, "What your family has done shapes your view of what is possible. Growing up seeing Grandma have so many plots of land and having so many houses made that a normal thing. That was absolutely something that was a reachable goal." Jendayi purchased her first house in Massachusetts while teaching at the Harvard Kennedy School of Government. When she moved to Washington, DC, she leased out her home in Massachusetts and has continuously leased it for over two decades. She said our grandparents shaped her view of property as an asset.

Another motivation for Jendayi to become a real estate investor was traveling to Omaha for Grandma's birthdays every year and seeing that many of our friends who lived in the Pratt Street neighborhood were leaving and moving further away from North Omaha. She wondered, "What's going on here?" She also observed that Warren Buffet had developed the downtown area close to the Near North Side and that development was pushing up taxes in North Omaha. She recognized a pattern, "I've seen this movie before, in Southeast DC [District of Columbia], where they just gentrified the whole place." She surmised, based on what she witnessed in DC, that "pretty soon, the Black people are going to be pushed out of the Near North Side." Jendayi had a front-row seat to the gentrification process in urban Black neighborhoods. She recalled, "I didn't like what I saw and wanted to do something about it."

Jendayi's evolution into real estate investment was also motivated by the reality that Black people's land ownership has always been in jeopardy. She said, "Black people need to keep their land in America." She recognized the scarcity of land and how "Black people have been pushed off of so much of our land," she said. This fact motivated her to hold on to our land and acquire more. Our grandparents gave her the confidence to step into the world of real estate investment and acquisition. Her own life experiences as a witness to gentrification fueled her resolve, and the legacy of systemic White resistance to Black property and land ownership steadied her focus on addressing the broader issue of Black inter-generational wealth attainment and accumulation.

Jendayi started investing in real estate in 2000 and owns rental properties and land to develop affordable housing in the United States. In 2015, she established BHW International LLC, the real estate subsidiary of her consulting and investment firm, 50 Ventures, LLC, founded in 2011. The mission of BHW International is to develop sustainable, affordable housing to support families with a quality life and a platform for generational wealth creation (50 Ventures, New Construction, 2024).

Acquiring the Pratt Street lots

Jendayi initially began to develop a portfolio of properties just as she learned of opportunities. However, she explained, "2801 Pratt Street was always a very special place, and when the city took it, that hurt. That really hurt." The city gave the property to the Omaha Municipal Land Bank (OMLB), a local, governmental non-profit corporation that takes vacant, abandoned, tax-delinquent, and dilapidated properties in Omaha and sells them to the high-est bidder (Omaha Land Bank, n.d.). Jendayi said, "One day, I was just looking at the properties listed by the OMLB, and there it was! I could not believe it! It was like a miracle, a blessing! There it was!" The 2801 Pratt Street lot was listed for sale by the OMLB.

Jendayi learned the OMLB process for acquiring property and put a bid on it. She was able to purchase the lot. She explained, "What happened with the land, because of new regulations, the setback was much deeper than when Grandma's house was there." This meant that the house Jendayi wanted to build on the lot could never be the size of Grandma and Grandpa's house. "It had to be a smaller house," she explained, "so in many ways, the land wasn't suitable for a house." Jendayi was told she could put a tiny house on the property or make it into a little park. She was not interested in making the land into a park, so she met with an architect to explore the possibility of building a little house but was not satisfied with that option either.

There were three other lots adjacent to the 2801 lot, and Jendayi realized that she would need to combine them all to build the house she envisioned. She bought one of the adjacent lots from Grandma, who still owned it. She asked her realtor to reach out to the owners of the other two lots, acting as her agent, and she eventually successfully acquired another lot adjacent to 2801. The last remaining lot took much longer to acquire. Jendayi explained,

> There are so many speculators trying to buy land in North Omaha that they are constantly writing letters and calling residents, and my realtor, who is White, was calling the owners of the last lot I wanted to buy. It was listed as North Eden Orchards. They wanted to give the land to some students at the local college.

Jendayi had the idea of approaching the students once they owned the land to see if she could buy it from them. Time passed without much happening in her attempt to purchase the third lot she needed to build a sizable house on the corner of 28th and Pratt Street.

Eventually, Jendayi's realtor learned that there was an unexpected death in the family of the owners of the third lot, and she suggested that Jendayi contact them directly. After the husband's death, his wife moved down South but told Jendayi that she wanted to honor what her husband wanted to do with the land and give it to the students at the local college, but she would talk to her adult children about it. After several months passed, Jendayi contacted the wife again, and by this time, she had moved to Maryland. During their second conversation, Jendayi said, "Maybe you knew my grandmother Berdine Williams," as she explained what she wanted to do with the property. The wife responded surprisingly, "Berdine Williams?!? We went to the same church! I love your grandmother! I was at her 100th birthday party!" Pleasantly surprised, Jendayi replied, "I was there too!" The wife invited Jendayi to her house for lunch and had a wonderful conversation. She and her sons were happy to sell the property to Jendayi.

The couple that owned the third lot were Drs. Jeffrey and Lillie Gayle Smith. They were longtime residents of North Omaha. Jeffrey enjoyed a 22-year career as an associate professor and director of school counseling in the Department of Education at Creighton University until his untimely death in June 2021. According to his obituary, he was "a servant of God and avid lover of nature [and] he developed North Eden Orchards, an urban fruit orchard [in Omaha] that shared nature's beauty and healthy foods with senior citizens and his neighbors" (Omaha World-Herald, 2021). Lillie is originally from Alabama, where she grew up picking cotton as a child in a field owned by her aunt, the previous owner being a Confederate captain (Smith, 2005). She earned a doctorate and taught.

Witnessing the health disparities in North Omaha, Lillie and her family decided to create a perpetual scholarship within Creighton's Health Sciences and Multicultural and Community Affairs Department (HS-MACA) to honor the life and legacy of her husband. The scholarship will assist graduate students of color with tuition toward degrees in medicine dentistry, pharmacy, and other health professions. The Smiths' generosity in selling the land to Jendayi and establishing the endowed scholarship supports the North Omaha community in two concrete ways: (1) with more affordable housing options and (2) with access to better health and longevity by increasing the availability of Black doctors to serve the community. According to research, Black people living in counties with Black doctors live longer (McFarling, 2023).

Educational preparation and funding

Jendayi realized the need for additional education to prepare herself better for the work she wanted to do in the real estate industry. She started by completing Rice University's eight-week Real Estate Investment and Development Executive Education course and earning her two-year MBA at The American University. Grandma often encouraged Jendayi as she prepared for her exams and other assignments. She frequently told Jendayi how confident she was in her ability to succeed and how proud she was of her for continuing her education.

Jendayi also enrolled in the Spark Academy real estate developer program in Omaha. The Academy's mission focuses on partnering with key stakeholders to transform disinvested neighborhoods into viable, thriving communities (Spark Academy, n.d.).

Part of the program curriculum involved meeting with key stakeholders, including banks, contractors, city officials, and planners, to network and explore potential partnerships.

50 Ventures Executive Assistant and CEO of Marketing and Communication, Ramona Durham, brought Jendayi's attention to Front Porch Investments several years prior, and it was one of the organizations Jendayi met at Spark Academy. She continued finetuning her real estate portfolio while acquiring the zoning, licensing, and other permits needed to become a viable competitor for real estate loans and grant opportunities targeting underserved, disinvested neighborhoods like North Omaha. While she did not receive the initial funding she applied for, Jendayi gained experience from each application process and improved her skills and portfolio. Subsequently, she successfully obtained a Front Porch Investment low-interest loan and a HOME Funds grant from the City of Omaha to build four affordable townhome rental properties on the corner of 2801 Pratt Street.

Jendayi explained that "affordability is calculated as a percentage of the average monthly income, from 30 per cent to 70 per cent. I decided to offer rent at the lowest level, 30 per cent, for the poorest families who will be housing voucher holders." Jendayi recognizes housing vouchers as an essential method to assist low-income families in gaining access to decent and safe housing in the private sector, consistent with the mission of BHW International. She plans to break ground on the construction of the townhomes in the spring and complete the units within 9 to 10 months.

An open-concept living design will be used, and each unit will have in-unit laundry. Jendayi believes,

> A decent home is a platform for everything, and the way I configured it, the two townhomes on the end are one-story, two bedrooms, two bathrooms, and fully accessible. They are for older adults or people living with a disability, and the two townhomes in the middle are two-story, three bedrooms, three bathrooms for families with children.

She continued, "I am trying to build that intergenerational environment we had growing up on Pratt Street, which creates healthy and resilient communities." Since the townhomes will be where our grandparents started their residential care home in 1954, the final step of the construction will be to install the original cornerstone in the building to honor them and their contributions and service to the North Omaha community.

Black people will continue to claim space, achieve success, create belonging, and affirm their lives to build economic, social, and cultural stability for themselves and successive generations. It is the essence of homemade citizenship. Similarly, it is the essence of White supremacy to respond to Black success with know-your-place aggression. Mitchell asserts, "Recognizing know-your-place aggression helps us stay clear about the actual cause-and-effect relationship that structures dominant culture. *Black success is the reason antiblackness became 'the weather'* [total climate]" (2020, p. 5).

Suggested discussion topics

1. If you had an opportunity to discuss legacy in your family, what would you talk about and with whom?

2. How do you think about Black history in America when you suspect that stories have been distorted? Are there stories in your family that you suspect are distorted? How do you recognize and address the misleading, inaccurate, slanted versions of the history of America and your family?

3. What are the differences between urban planning, redevelopment, and gentrification, and the implications for people living in urban spaces?

4. How is racially coded language used in your experience?

5. Reflecting on Mitchell's concepts of homemade citizenship and know-your-place aggression, what examples of these phenomena have you witnessed in your lifetime?

References

50 Ventures. (2024). *BHW International*. [Online] Available at: www.50ventures.com/bhw [Accessed 29 Jan. 2024].

American National Bank. (n.d.). *American National Bank—Carver Legacy Center joint venture*. [Online] Available at: www.american. bank/carver-legacy-center/ [Accessed 14 Jan. 2024].

Anderson, C. (2016). *White Rage: The Unspoken Truth of Our Racial Divide*. New York, NY: Bloomsbury.

Archer, D. N. (2020). "White Men's Roads Through Black Men's Homes": Advancing Racial Equity Through Highway Reconstruction. *Vanderbilt Law Review*, 73(5), pp. 1259–1330.

Archer, D. N. (2021). Transportation Policy and the Underdevelopment of Black Communities. *Iowa Law Review*, 106, pp. 2125–2151.

Bailey, A. C. (2017). *The Weeping Time: Memory and the Largest Slave Auction in American History*. New York: Cambridge University Press.

Barnes, K. C. (2004). *Journey of Hope: The Back-to-Africa Movement in Arkansas*. Chapel Hill: The University of North Carolina Press.

Carter, R. L. (2014). Valued Lives in Violent Places: Black Urban Placemaking at a Civil Rights Memorial in New Orleans. *City & Society*, 26(2), pp. 239–261.

City of Omaha Recovery Plan. (2022). *State and local fiscal recovery funds: 2022 report*. [Online] Available at: https://home.treasury. gov/system/files/136/Omaha_2022RecoveryPlan_SLT-1682.pdf [Accessed 19 Jan. 2024].

Emberton, C. (2017). "Cleaning up the mess": Some thoughts on freedom, violence, and grief. In: D. W. Blight and J. Downs, eds.,

Beyond Freedom: Disrupting the History of Emancipation. Athens, GA: The University of Georgia Press, pp. 136–144.

Emberton, C. (2022). *To Walk About in Freedom: The Long Emancipation of Priscilla Joyner.* New York: W.W. Norton & Company.

Encyclopedia of Arkansas (2024). *Elaine Massacre of 1919.* [Online]. Available at: https://encyclopediaofarkansas.net/entries/elaine-massacre-of-1919-1102/# [Accessed 13 Feb. 2023].

Equal Justice Initiative, (2020) Reconstruction in America: Racial Violence after the Civil War, 1865–1876. Montgomery: Equal Justice Initiative.

Federal Writers' Project. (1939). *Nebraska: A Guide to the Cornhusker State.* Nebraska State Historical Society. New York: The Viking Press.

Feimster, C. N. (2005). How are the daughters of Eve punished? Rape during the Civil War. In: E. A. Payne, ed., *Writing Women's History: A Tribute to Anne Firor Scott.* Jackson: University of Mississippi Press, pp. 64–81.

Fotsch, P. M. (2007). *Watching the Traffic Go By: Transportation and Isolation in Urban America.* Austin: University of Texas Press.

Front Porch Investments (n.d.) *Who we are.* [Online] Available at: https://frontporchinvestments.org [Accessed 21 Jan. 2024].

Geter, H. A. (2022). *The Black Period: On Personhood, Race, and Origin.* New York: Random House.

Gordon, F. L. (1993). From slavery to uncertain freedom: Blacks in the delta. In: J. Whayne and W. B. Gatewood, eds., *The Arkansas Delta: Land of Paradox.* Fayetteville: The University of Arkansas Press, pp. 98–127.

Hartman, S. (2008). Venus in Two Acts. *Small Axe*, 12(2), pp. 1–14. Available at: https://doi.org/10.1215/-12-2-1 [Accessed 24 Feb. 2022].

Hine, D. C. (1989). *Black Women in White: Racial Conflict and Cooperation in the Nursing Profession 1890–1950*. Bloomington: Indiana University Press.

Horowitz, R. (1997). Negro and White, Unite and Fight!: A Social History of Industrial Unionism in Meatpacking, 1930–90. Urbana and Chicago: University of Illinois Press.

Jones-Hannah, N. (2021). Justice. In: N. Hannah-Jones, C. Roper, I. Silverman, and J. Silverstein, eds., *The 1619 Project: A New Origin Story*. New York: One World, pp. 451–476.

Jones-Rogers, S. E. (2019). *They Were Her Property: White Women as Slave Owners in the American South*. New Haven: Yale University Press.

Kephart, B. (2021). House as Home: Writing the Places That Raised Us. *Brevity: A Journal of Concise Literary Nonfiction* (n.v./n.p.). Available at: https://brevitymag.com/craft-essays/writing-the-places/ [Accessed 14 July 2023].

Kotoz, C. David. (August 17, 1983). "Development or Decay?: Hopes, Doubts Mix on North Side." Omaha World-Herald, No. 3,

Matkin-Rawn, S. (2013). "The Great Negro State of the Country": Arkansas Reconstruction and the Other Great Migration. *The Arkansas Historical Quarterly*, 72(1), pp. 1–41.

McFarling, U. L. (2023). In counties with more Black doctors, Black people live longer, "astonishing" study finds. *Stat News* (n.v./n.p) [Online]. Available at: www.statnews.com/2023/04/14/black-doctors-primary-care-life-expectancy-mortality/ [Accessed 30 Jan. 2024].

McKinney, T. and Wayne, J. T. (2022). *North Omaha Recovery Plan 2022–2025: State and Local Fiscal Recovery Funds & General Funds*, pp. 1–40. Available at: https://northomaha2022.com [Accessed 14 Jan. 2024].

Mitchell, K. (2020). *From Slave Cabins to the White House: Homemade Citizenship in African American Culture*. Chicago, IL: University of Illinois Press.

Morrison, T. (2008). *What Moves at the Margins: Selected Nonfiction*. Jackson: University Press of Mississippi.

Omaha Municipal Land Bank (n.p.). *What we do*. [Online] Available at: https://omahalandbank.org/what-we-do/ [Accessed 21 Jan. 2024].

Omaha World-Herald (February 2, 1979). Nursing home built on a foundation of caring. NewsBank.

Omaha World-Herald (June 13, 2021). Obituaries. [Online]. Available at: www.legacy.com/us/obituaries/omaha/name/jeff rey-smith-obituary?id=5774995 [Accessed 30 Jan. 2024].

Pospisil, Stu (2021). Omaha's south side was always more than its nicknames. *Omaha World-Herald* (n.v.), p. E2. Available at: https:// infoweb.newsbank.com/apps/news/document-view?p=AMN EWS&docref=news/1862936B9D1BDBC8 [Accessed 27 Nov. 2023].

Rable, G. C. (2007). *But There Was No Peace: The Role of Violence in the Politics of Reconstruction*. Athens, GA: The University of Georgia Press.

Robertson, I., and Rogers, W. A. (1938). *Federal Writers' Project— Arkansas Slave Narrative Collection*. Works Progress Administration. New York: Firework Press.

Sanchez, L. (2021). Omaha's Black history: How well do you know the history of your city? Today's news is inextricably linked to our past. *The Reader*. (n.v./n.p.). [Online] Available at: https:// thereader.com/2021/02/16/omahas-black-history/ [Accessed 14 Jan. 2024].

Scoop. (2004). The good ole days. *The Omaha Star*, 66 (36).

Sharpe, C. (2023). *Ordinary Notes*. New York: Farrar, Straus, and Giroux.

Smith, L. G. (2005). Unearthing hidden literacy: Seven lessons I learned in a cotton field. In: J. K. Dowdy, ed., *Readers of the Quilt: Essays on Being Black, Female, and Literate*. Cresskill, NJ: Hampton Press. pp. 39–46.

Spark Academy (n.d.) *Spark's mission*. [Online] Available at: www.sparkcdi.org/our-approach [Accessed 31 Jan. 2024].

Stockley, G. (n.d.). Elaine Massacre of 1919. In: *Encyclopedia of Arkansas*. Little Rock: The Butler Center for Arkansas Studies, n.p. Available at: https://encyclopediaofarkansas.net/entries/elaine-massacre-of-1919-1102/ [Accessed 10 Feb. 2023].

Trammell, J. (2012). *The Richmond Slave Trade: The Economic Backbone of the Old Dominion*. Stroud, UK: The History Press.

United States Department of Transportation Federal Highway Administration and Nebraska Department of Roads (1975).

Valandra. (2012). Reflexivity and Professional Use of Self in Research: A Doctoral Student's Journey. *Journal of Ethnographic and Qualitative Research*, 6(4), pp. 204–220.

Valandra, and Leslie, T. (2022). The history of incarceration of African Americans/Blacks in the United States. In: K. Johns, ed., *Counseling Strategies for Children and Families Impacted by Incarceration*. Hershey, PA: IGI Global Publishers, pp. 24–46.

Vireo. (2021). *Forever North: Housing and Multimodal Transportation Strategy*. Chicago, IL: Applied Real Estate.

Warren, W. J. (1996). The Impasse of Racialism and Race: Omaha's Meatpacking Unionism, 1945–1955. *Journal of the West*, 35, pp. 50–54.

Winkler, I. (2018). Doing Autoethnography: Facing Challenges, Taking Choices, Accepting Responsibilities. *Qualitative Inquiry*, 24(4), pp. 236–247.

Woldoff, R. (2011). *White Flight/Black Flight: The Dynamics of Racial Change in an American Neighborhood*. Ithaca, NY: Cornell University Press.

Further reading

Theories

Crenshaw, K., Gotanda, N., Peller, G., and Thomas, K. eds. (1995). *Critical Race Theory: The Key Writings That Formed the Movement*. New York: The New Press.

Waites, C. (2009). *Social Work Practice with African American Families: An Intergenerational Perspective*. New York, NY: Routledge.

Research methods

Datta, R., and Chapola, J. (2023). Decolonizing autoethnography. In: J. M. Okoko and K. D. Walker, eds., *Varieties of Qualitative Research Methods*. Springer Cham.: Springer Texts in Education, pp. 121–126. Available at: https://doi.org/10.1007/978-3-031-04394-9_20 [Accessed 25 Aug. 2023].

Racialized urban housing and transportation policy

Moskowitz, P. E. (2018). *How to Kill a City: Gentrification, Inequality, and the Fight for the Neighborhood*. New York: Bold Type Books.

Taylor, K-Y. (2019). *Race for Profit: How Banks and the Real Estate Industry Undermined Black Homeownership*. Chapel Hill: The University of North Carolina Press.

Race and racism

Hardy, K. V. (2022). *The Enduring Invisibility and Ubiquitous Centrality of Whiteness*. New York: W.W. Norton & Company.

Hardy, K.V. (2023). *Racial Trauma: Clinical Strategies and Techniques for Healing Invisible Wounds*. New York: W.W. Norton & Company.

Index

1619 Project, *The* (Hannah-Jones) 37

Adams Park 123

African American; entrepreneurial opportunities 137; meatpacking workers 46; newspapers 97; oral tradition 14; residents 132; state senator 132; traditions 3; treatment by northern soldiers 17; White people confined 36; youth in North Omaha 133

African emigration movement 21

African Methodist Episcopal (AME) Church 29

Alcornled, James 19

American Rescue Plan Act (ARPA) 137

anti-black 177; racism 102

anti-Black; violence 114

Archer, D. N 131

Arkansas 1, 3, 31, 147, 162; grandmother left 2; rural community 8; rural, migration form 3

Arkansas Delta 20

ARPA. *See* American Rescue Plan Act

ARPA funds 138

Asian population 105

Aust, Alden 136

Autobiography of Miss Jane Pittman, The (film) 83

autoethnography 7

Barnes, K. C 21

Bass, Karen 156

Bergan Mercy Medical Center 148

Bermuda 118

BHW International LLC 180

Black Americans 13, 120, 177; political shifts 21

Black Baptist church 126

Black bodies 114

Black body 104

Black Box 39

Black care 114

Black church 32, 97, 114

Black communities 23, 114, 118, 131, 138, 185; Arkansas

20; attacking and killing 19; construction 112; depiction in film industry 112; destruction 133; formerly enslaved 19; home-owning 106; Near North Side 36; restricted to Near North Side 132; social value 35; spiritual needs 102; stereotypical representations 111; working-class 3

Black community 82

Black dirt makeshift court 84

Black doctors 183

Black employees 124

Black employment 31

Black families 4, 38, 102, 118, 122; descendant survived in Elaine Massacre 26; escape white racial violence 22; leaving South 31; low-income 120; middle-class 106; North Omaha 7, 36, 37; wealth gap and 106; working-class 120

Black farmers 20, 26

Black folks 112

Black human geography 14, 35

Black land and homeowners 37, 123

Black life 121; freedom 114; negative stereotypes 112; negative stories 104; offensive representations 4; segregated spaces 115; textbooks' stories 5; urban 6

Black middle-class families 106

Black midwives and nurses 50

Black migration 20

Black national anthem 35

black neighborhood; urban 112

Black neighborhood 5, 37, 92, 134; North Omaha 58; urban 179

Black notes 113, 115

Black Period 104–05

Black Republicans 19

Black spaces 114, 123

Black urban bodies 36

Black urban life, deficit-based framing 4–9

Black urban place-making 4

Black urban spaces 4, 115

Black Wall Street 36

Black women 19, 49, 51, 117; agency of 8; in white space 117; public rape of 18

Black working-class 5

Black-on-Black crime 127

Black-owned financial institution 38

Blondo Street house 32, 40, 41

Bobby Williams 148

BrightStarCare 167

Brown, Willis 113

Carter Lake 74

CEF. See child evangelism fellowship

certified nursing aid (CNA) 152

Chambers, Ernie 132

Charles Drew Health Center 53

child evangelism fellowship (CEF) 101

church 87. *See also* Religion

CIO. *See* Congress of Industrial Organizations

city disinvestment 4

Civic Nebraska 113

Civil War 14, 16, 31

Claire Methodist Church 83

comfortable neighborhood 103

Congress of Industrial Organizations (CIO) 45

Cottage, Richard 120

Covid-19 pandemic lockdown 169

critical fabulation method 8

Czech settlers 100

Davis, Charles F 38

death and grieving 67–69

Dots and Tots 119

Druid Hill 85

Durham, Ramona 184

East Side, West Side (CBS series) 83

Elaine Massacre of 1919 25–27

Elliott, RoAnne 151, 166, 167, 170, 171

Emberton, Carole 13, 31

enslaved South 14–19

enslavement 102; Black people in Arkansas 20; Richmond, Virginia 13; South 14

Ewing, John 122

family space 59, 62

family values 90–95

Federal Home Owners Lending Corporation 39

Federal Housing Act 37

Federal Housing Administration (FHA) program 37

Federal Writers' Project (FWP) 8

Feimster, C. N 18

Fontanelle Elementary School 101

Forever North Omaha Project 139

Franklin Elementary 35

Frazer, Ida 9

Frazer, Jendayi 31, 34, 63, 150, 156; acquiring Pratt Street lots 180–83; educational preparation and funding 183; inheritance and legacy 177–80; real estate investment 179–80; sworn as US Ambassador to South Africa 155

Friars Point 22; Union troops used 18

Friars Point, Mississippi 15

Front Porch Investments 184

Front Porch Investments (FPI) 138

FWP. *See* Federal Writers'; Project

Gabrielle Union Pond 123

gentrification 106

gentrification, Hill, Linda 119–28

Geter, H. A 104

Gibson, Bridget 169

Goodwin, Alvin 120

Goose Hollow 99

Grace Bible College 99

Grandparents' Day 172–75

Great Depression 28

Hall, Dennis 24, 29, 37; children 26; death 30; surviving child 31

Hall, Eleanor 24

Hall, Ida Henderson 15, 23, 144, 147; children 24, 26; death 31; land purchased by 30–31; longest-living child 174; worked as domestic worker 28

Hall, Monroe 24

Hannah-Jones, Nikole 37

Hartman, Saidiya 7

Health—Immanuel Fontenelle Rehabilitation Institute 148

health disparities 183

Health Sciences and Multicultural and Community Affairs Department (HS-MACA) 183

Henderson, James 146, 147

Henderson, Larissa 146

Henderson, Lizzie 19, 23

Henderson, Sherman 19, 23

Hester, Ephram 16, 18

Hill, Linda 117–28; childhood 123; housing and gentrification 119–28; lost equity in home 122; member of Zion Baptist Church 126; moved to North Omaha 118–19; openness and courage 118; professional life 124–25; spiritual faith 126–27

Holy Name Church 119

Holy Name Elementary School 125

HOME Funds 184

homemade citizenship 177, 178

Horace Mann 85

hospice chaplain 173

hospice services 167

housing discrimination 2, 37, 39

Housing Program funds 138

housing segregation 4

housing, Hill, Linda 119–28

Immanuel Fontenelle Rehabilitation Institute 149

Jackson, Jesse 119

Jean, Bobbie 32

Jendayi; Barbara taught hair style to 83

Jim Crow 166

Jim Crow Emerson, Arkansas 79

Jim Crow era 27, 50

Jim Crow laws; institution of 21

Jim Crow South 6, 14, 24–25

Johnson, J. Rosamond 35

Johnson, James Weldon 35

Johnson, Lizzie Spotsell 13, 14, 175; persuaded to go to Helena, Arkansas 20; shared her life story with Willie An 15–16

Jones-Rogers, S. E 17

Kelly's Drugstore 33, 70, 93

Kent, Mose 16–17; arrived in Mississippi 18

Kephart, B 13

Keyes, Calvin 168, 172

King, Martin Luther 113

Klan violence 27

Kotok, C. David 133

Ku Klux Klansmen 127

LaBelle, Patti 169

Lake Fayetteville 169

Lampkin, Cornelia 30, 161–64

Lampkin, Homer P 30

land purchase 30–31

Larry's Station 33

Lassiter, Ralph 139, 148, 155

Latino family 101

Leahy, Eugene 136

Liberia 21, 22

Long Elementary School 40

Love, Preston, Jr 132

McGettis, Neale 29

McMillan, Jannie 30

middle-class 85; Black communities 110; home-owning, Black community 106; neighborhood 107

Morris, Craig 38

Morrison, Toni 7

Mount Hope cemetery 90

Mount Nebo Baptist Church 144

Mount Pisgah 98

Mount Moriah Baptist Church 6, 32, 41, 46, 70, 139, 154, 156; merged with Risen Son Baptist Churches 97; Mount Pisgah developed into 98

Myers Funeral Home 126

Near North Side 119, 120, 121, 136, 179; Black community 132; neglecting 135

Nebraska 32

neighborhood 88, 105; 28th Street 90; Black 92, 134; changing 108; comfortable 103; contrast of 85–89; formerly redlined 138;

middle-class 107; North Omaha 110, 122; Pratt Street 164; Reddick 88, 90; Tarver family 80–82; White 159

New Deal policy 28

New Era Baptist State Convention 113

New Orleans 15

North Eden Orchards 181, 182

North Freeway 79, 82, 119, 131–39, 178; construction 132; history 131–35; perceptions 133–35; planning and disinvestment 135–37; proposed pathway 132

North Omaha 35; African American youth in 133; Ames in 6; Black church in 32; Black community 7; Black families and neighborhoods in 37; Black families in 36; Black workers segregated in 45; Black working-class neighborhood in 33; community 101; experiences and memories of living in 5; health disparities in 183; history of 33–54; Latino family in 101; Linda moved to 118–19; media representations 110; modern 102–05; negative perception of 113; neighborhood 34; North 24th Street 36; residents of 3, 8; roots of 36; traditional 104; White people's perceptions of 114; working-class Black community of 3

nursing home business 69

Omaha 1, 2; Black investment in 137; daycare center in 119; grandparents moved to 35; Near North Side of 32; racial tensions in 45; racism in 45

Omaha Chamber of Commerce 123

Omaha City Council 53, 123

Omaha Economic Development Corporation 120

Omaha Municipal Land Bank (OMLB) 180

Omaha Public Power District (OPPD) 124, 125

Omaha riots 119

Omaha Star, The 34

Omaha Together One Community 102

Omaha World-Herald 135, 136

OMLB See Omaha Municipal Land Bank

open-concept living design 185

OPPD See Omaha Public Power District

Ordinary Notes (Sharpe) 114

Pacific Springs Village 157

packing plant industry 45

Packinghouse Workers Organizing Committee (PWOC) 45

Partee, Richard 172

Pastor Williams. *See* Williams, T. Michael

patients; grandparents caring for 60–63; like family 63–67; privacy 66

planned urban renewal/removal project 76–77

polio epidemic 52

Pospisil, Stu 99

Pratt Street house 1, 6, 42, 53, 58–60, 69; converted to licensed residential care 2; landscape outside 74; Nelson protector outside 70–71; planned urban removal project 76–77; relationship to 3; remembering 178

Pratt Street neighborhood 33, 135, 163, 179

Prison Industrial Complex 112

Prospect Hill Cemetery 48, 49, 50

public Black spaces 123

public white space 118

PWOC *See* Packinghouse Workers Organizing Committee

racial prejudice 2, 118

racial violence; through Reconstruction 6; white 22

racism 2, 4; in Omaha 45; structural 37

reconstruction; after Civil War 27

Reconstruction; South 19–21

Reddick Street 93

redevelopment project 138

Rice, Condoleezza 155

Risen Son Baptist Church 100

Robertson, Irene 14, 15, 18, 22, 23

Rogers, Willie Ann 8, 9, 14; birth record 14–15; Brinkley 23; family ended up in Brinkley 22; Friars Point 18; FWP interview 13

Roosevelt, Franklin D 28

rural farm community, Monroe County 14

Sayers, Anna 24

Senator Council 133

sharecropping 26, 27–28

Sharpe, C 114, 115

Shelley, Anne 169

Sherman, William T 19

Shukert, Marty 136

Singleton, Jim 18

slavery 27

Smith, Harriet 41–44

Smith, Paul 41–44

Smith, Ruby 81

Smith, Sidney 81

South; enslaved 14–19; Jim Crow 24–25; reconstruction 19–21

South Omaha 38; culture 99–102; ethnic European congregation in 100

Southside Baptist Church 99

Southview Baptist Church 100

Spark Academy 183

Spencer Street 93

spiritual faith 126–27

spirituality, values 115

St John's African Methodist Episcopal church 126

Stothert, Jean 123

Swift & Company 31, 32, 44, 46

Swift Packing Plant 32, 44

Tarver family 79–95, 119, 178; abandoning roots 82; contrast neighborhoods 85–89; neighborhood 80–82; values 90–95

Tarver, Barbara 79, 84, 89, 91–92, 93, 95; taught hairstyle 83

Tarver, Caroline 79

Tarver, Howard, Jr 79

Tarver, Johnny 79

Tarver, Mae Della 79

Tarver, Milton 79, 83–84, 88, 89, 90, 91, 92, 93, 94; home 82; racial disparities faced by 86; transferred to Northwest High School 86

Tarver, Susie 79, 82, 88, 90, 92; connected to spiritual community 87; started college 87

Tech High 118, 123

Ten Commandments 127

The Weeping Time: Memory and the Largest Slave Auction in American History (Bailey) 16

Tulsa Rising Museum 135

Tyson, Cicely 83

Union Pacific Railroad 124

Union soldiers; conventional narratives 17; entered Richmond 14, 16

United Meatpacking Workers of America 46

United Packinghouse Workers of America; workers 46

United Packinghouse Workers of America (UPWA) 45

University of Arkansas 147

University of Nebraska 6, 24, 87; Lifelong Learning Initiative's Program for Women and Successful Aging 143

UPWA See United Packinghouse Workers of America

violence, racial 25–28

Voting Rights Act of 1965 166

Warren, Theresa 29

White; folks 28, 46, 50, 53, 113; landowners 26, 27;

meatpacking workers 44; neighborhood 159; supremacy 19, 25, 37, 118, 185; terrorism 21; West Omaha 118

White financial and real estate institutions 37

William, Howard, Sr 79

Williams Care Manor 2, 25, 53–54

Williams Residential Care Home 54, 57–77; death and grieving 67–69; patients 60–63; patients like family 63–67

Williams, Berdine Hall 1–3, 8, 141–75; 101st birthday celebration 171; as "Sister Williams" 64; assisted living 157–61; birthday 142; birthday cards 171–72; care of White children 30; care plan 158; caregivers 159; celebrating 100th birthday 154–57; death 3; family visits 172–75; favorite foods 155; fell down and surgery 148–54; joy and gratitude 164; living and working in her 90s 142–48; marriage and migration of 31–32; patient privacy 66; physical therapy 152; rehabilitation 152–54; returned to Arkansas 166–69; signs of memory loss 159; special events 170–72; spelling classes 29; turned 90 143; visiting Mrs Lampkin 161–64; worked as nurse

49–50; work ethic and motto 3; worked on family farm 27

Williams, Bobbie Jean 144, 148

Williams, Bobby Hall 1; "work worries" 44; and boning knife 46–48; church deacon at Mount Moriah 75; death 68; grave site 48; marriage and migration 31–32; work and play 73–76; worked in Swift Packing Plant 44–48

Williams, Doris 3, 9, 32, 44, 143, 144, 145, 165; plots 49; rented car garage 38–39

Williams, Kinze 32

Williams, Nelson 48, 49, 50, 61, 68–69, 148; death 68–69; funeral 69; in hospital 68; intellectual capacity 71; physical limitations 71; protector outside Pratt Street house 70–71

Williams, T Michael 97–115, 122, 133, 134, 135, 138, 178; media representation 110; ministry and South Omaha culture 99–102; modern North Omaha and 102–05; part of Mount Moriah 97; shifting demographics and safety 105–15

working-class 37, 45, 58; communities 5; families 106; renters 106

Works Progress Administration (WPA) 9; and education 28–32

worship houses 34

Yaeger family 49

Yaeger, Alice M 48, 49, 50

Yaeger, Barney E 48

Yaeger, Mathilda E 48

YMCA 117

Zion 97

Zion Baptist Church 126